The Wye Plays

The Back of Beyond

and

The Battle of the Crows

David Ian Rabey

intellect™
Bristol, UK
Portland, OR, USA

First published in UK in 2004 by
Intellect Books, PO Box 862, Bristol BS99 1DE, UK

First published in USA in 2004 by
Intellect Books, ISBS, 920 NE 58th Ave. Suite 300, Portland, Oregon 97213-3786, USA

Series Editor: Roberta Mock
Copy Editor: Julie Strudwick
Front cover photograph by Keith Morris: Hannah Oakey as Wye in *The Back of Beyond*.
Cover design: Paul Prudden.

A catalogue record for this book is available from the British Library

ISBN 1-84150-115-8

Printed in Great Britain by Antony Rowe Ltd.

Contents

Acknowledgements

'On Being a Shakespearian Dramatist: An Approach to *The Back of Beyond*', by David Ian Rabey, was originally published in *Theatre Research International*, volume 25, number 3 (Autumn 2000), and is reproduced by permission of Cambridge University Press.

Thanks to series editor Roberta Mock for her efforts on behalf of these plays.

Diolch:
To Keith Morris and Andy Freeman for their generous permission to reproduce their splendid production photographs.
To Lurkers past present and future: *ni yma o hyd*, and I love you madly;
And to the Lurking Truth/Gwir sy'n Llechu management board, especially the Atomic Mr Chairman.

THE BACK OF BEYOND

By David Ian Rabey

What are we to make of the strangers we are to each other and to ourselves?

Brendan Kennelly, *The Trojan Women*

I've run out of reasons for keeping it neat

Becker & Fagen, *Ida Lee*

And that's true too

King Lear, V.2.

Dedicated to Roger Owen, Eric Schneider and Charmian Savill, who admitted the consequences...

1

On Being a Shakespearian Dramatist:

An Approach to The Back of Beyond

David Ian Rabey

> *The lack of constant speech is not contempt*
> *But silence measures those compelled to speak.*
> *What does not change is will to change, they say,*
> *Though changes do outrun the will's control.*
> *Each person has a story that rolls on*
> *Beyond the boundaries of the play in which they're placed,*
> *Unless they fall in love at last with limits*
> *And try to die into an old play's shape.*
> *Not even witches know what happens after,*
> *But once I met an actor, wild and broken,*
> *Who said, 'The play is dead: long live the play', with laughter,*
> *Then wept at faces he saw in the bracken.*

So speaks the witch named Wye, anti-heroine of my plays *The Back of Beyond* (staged 1996) and *The Battle of the Crows* (staged 1998). Thus she associates the death wish of exhaustion with an impulse to subside into a predetermined dramatic form, whereas life pushes on beyond all man-made boundaries and limitations of definition. Nevertheless, the actor of whom she speaks is powerfully, compulsively self-contradictory. He discovers himself bound to acknowledge melancholy - cracked and haunted by the sensed inevitability of irrevocable loss - even as he heralds the equal inevitability of the next transformation which he will embody, in demonstration of the spirit of wild laughter. This self-consciously and deliberately riven figure might also serve as a paradigm for a Shakespearian dramatist, such as I attempt to be.

At this point, you may think, or even object, that even to harbour the temerity to consider the ambition of being a Shakespearian dramatist is arrogant, hubristic and pretentious. I would counter as follows: it is not arrogant to admit, or even to proclaim, a profound influence and inspiration; and that the identification of that influence does not propose an equality or even a similarity but points to a dialogue which invites further negotiation by others, and thus strives to transcend a potentially disastrous isolation. And any art, but particularly dramatic art, externalizes inner life in a way which might justly be termed pretentious, in that it bids to manifest an unusual and unconventional (if not always enviable) sensitivity to something, attempting to identify transcendent things in the everyday, expanding the narrow vocabulary of being which is afforded by literal description of objectified facts. The question is: how well does it realize its pretentions by challenging imaginatively a dominant discourse of sterile presumption? The theatre is not a place for false modesty, or a monument to pseudo-egalitarian functionalism: it is always being specifically artificial, and I would even suggest that this is what human beings do best.

Howard Barker has noted how Shakespeare is 'now a negligible influence on the tone of contemporary writing in Britain' and how this situation is 'itself a tragedy for the theatre of our time'; rather, the uncontested authority of Chekhov in British theatrical and cultural circles 'has made of him a more luminous icon in this part of Europe than even in his country of origin'.[i] The effect of this, as I have noted elsewhere,[ii] is an enshrinement of 'realism' expressed as conformity in objectified defeat, in order to deny the socially unmanageable individual capacity for unpredictable self-transformation. The purposefully metaphorical drama practiced by Barker, David Rudkin and myself is deliberately opposed to such supposedly inevitable confinements. Barker explains how his divergent exploration of Shakespeare's tragedy, *Seven Lears* (1990), grew from 'a writer's feeling for the architecture of a text, and we have slowly re-learned that architecture is about emptiness as well as substance, void as well as materiality'.[iii] This intuition reverberates into Peter Holland's observation: 'Action, the physical event that Shakespeare incompletely prescribes, becomes a necessary choice at each and every moment of performance, one choice inevitably excluding many others.'[iv] The genius of Shakespeare's drama might aptly be said to reside in the *incompleteness* of its *prescriptions*: hence its challenging power and infinitely renewing fascination. I would add that the 'necessary choice' of the dramatist, like that of the performer, also excludes, yet somehow simultaneously illuminates, others. My play *The Back of Beyond* marinaded in my unconscious through my fascination for Shakespeare's play, an admiration of the 'Lear plays' by Barker, Bond and Rudkin (*The Saxon Shore*), and also because of an instinctive drive to interrogate the material differently, and to pursue the different consequences which might be seismically triggered. Shakespeare may have been institutionalized, canonized and abstracted into a national icon for purposes of tourism and commerce, but he is also a dramatist who is enliveningly dangerous and therefore important to learn from. The best directors approach his work with respect, but not with deference to a notional stability; dramatists might well do the same. 'Fear is a pretty sceptre but a useless tool', says Echternacht, another character in *The Back of Beyond*, of whom I will tell more later. It is worth reminding ourselves in this context that this is how Shakespeare himself usually worked. With the exceptions of the apparently 'sourceless' plays (*Love's Labour's Lost*, *A Midsummer Night's Dream* and *The Tempest*), every Shakespeare play is a consciously surprising re-emphasizing re-animation of some pre-existing story or play, and the explosive power of *King Lear* is amplified by its startling final departure from the happy ending of its chrysalis play, *King Leir*.

The first germination of *The Back of Beyond* perhaps occurred in Berkeley in 1979, where, as a graduate student on a travel scholarship to the University of California, I attended the M.A. colloquia of Stephen Booth, who was developing some of the ideas which would feature in his book, *'King Lear', 'Macbeth', Indefinition and Tragedy* (1983). These were not traditional colloquia, more philosophical-psychological workshops in the form of intellectual cliffhangers approached at escape velocity in order to split conceptual atoms, and the most exciting times in my formally directed education. The group sessions basically required those involved to take their senses of their own sanity on a series of kamikaze missions exposed by Shakespeare's tragedies: the possible 'necessity of recognizing that what makes sense may not be true'.[v] Part of Booth's reading of *King Lear* might be summarized thus:

> I submit that audiences are not shocked by the fact of Cordelia's death but by its situation and that audiences grieve not for Cordelia's physical vulnerability, or for the physical vulnerability of humankind, but for their own - our own - mental vulnerability, a vulnerability made absolutely inescapable when the play pushes inexorably beyond its own identity, rolling across and crushing the very framework that enables its audience to endure the otherwise terrifying explosion of all manner of ordinarily indispensable mental contrivances for isolating, limiting and comprehending. When Lear enters howling in the last moments of the play, Shakespeare has already presented an action that is serious, of undoubted magnitude, *and complete*; he thereupon continues that action beyond the limits of the one category that no audience can expect to see challenged: Shakespeare presents the culminating events of his *story* after his *play* is over.[vi]

Booth notes how, for all 'the characters constantly and vainly strive to establish the limits of things', 'not ending is a primary characteristic of *King Lear* and, hence, 'the intensity of patterning in *King Lear* compensates for the equal intensity of its demonstration that the characters', the audience's and all human perception is folly'.[vii] It was from him that I learnt that the most centrally purposeful line of *King Lear* might be: 'And that's true too.'

In 1982, I watched Adrian Noble's RSC production of *King Lear* four times, profoundly disturbed and riveted by the performances of Antony Sher as The Fool and Jonathan Hyde as Edgar in particular. Both characterizations seemed to confront and respond to the demonic aspects of the characters, more usually tamed or ignored. Sher's chilling, crippled, Grock-like mongrel discovered a brief epiphany of supernatural release in proclaiming and physicalizing the Albion speech which concludes with the psychic hand-grenade of a line: 'This prophecy Merlin shall make, for I live before his time.' As Edgar, Hyde suggested an alternately cool and wracked chameleon, a deliberate tactician who could strategically render himself into the shape of a monstrosity of suffering. He seemed most disturbingly and bleakly knowing when Edgar's surprising and oddly autonomous psychic construction of Poor Tom was discarded and stigmatized as a vicious fiend, in order to support the illusion of a benign cosmology which we, as his implicated audience, know to be merely the illusion generated by an experiential experiment in invisible theatre.

Later that year, my career as a full-time lecturer began with a temporary appointment in English and Drama at the University of Dublin, Trinity College. With his permission, I quote some words from an essay by Ron Callan, one of the students in my first seminar group on Shakespeare's Tragedies:

> Lear gropes his way back to the fixed center of order, but this is not within himself (as

5

it is in Edgar) but centered in Cordelia; and in this play external images (especially superlatives) are fated to fail to sustain life. Through Lear we experience chaos; Edgar, Kent, the Fool and Cordelia help him make the journey; Edgar (with his tendency to shy away from important sensations) alone help us to hold that experience.[viii]

Whilst the events of the play force Edgar to witness and respond to extremity, he maintains a faith that his own powers of performance can form and frame an ultimately cogent (if apparently chaotic) response. However, it remains a moot point as to which is the *external* image: his social persona of well-meaning but ineffectual young nobleman, or the adopted guise of Bedlam beggar; and, indeed, how far this can 'sustain life'.[ix]

Cut to Gregynog Hall, mid-Wales, in 1993, where I'm a tutor on a weekend residential Creative Writing course, and I set the students a spontaneous writing exercise: one agrees on the basis that I undertake the exercise myself. I discover in myself the voice of the compulsively performative yet ultimately inscrutable Edgar, considering his future, his options and his sexuality in a way in which he is not permitted in Shakespeare's play. I find that the library of this increasingly gothic edifice can furnish me with a folio copy of the apocryphal *King Leir* - disappointing apart from a couple of resonant images and an intriguing emphasis on more deliberate cruelty from Leir to Cordella. But then I turn to Holinshed and Geoffrey of Monmouth. Both chronicles extend the story of Lear's family beyond his death and burial at Leicester, and tell how Cordelia was restored to Lear only to survive him, but then to die of despair when subsequently imprisoned by Goneril and Regan's sons - both conscious exclusions from Shakespeare's story. The chronicles give various accounts of the rivalry arising between these two cousins, and of the spelling of their names (I settled on the variants Cundah and Morgan) but agree that one pursued the other to Wales and killed him, but thereafter named the area after him. This fractal spread of speculative possibilities struck me as disturbingly subversive a narrative premise in relation to Shakespeare's *King Lear*, as that play has been to the original *King Leir*. Shakespeare's subversion of a once-familiar story extends horror and uncertainty beyond the conventional generic markers of tragedy and drama. I reflected that a further extrapolation of the story into a separate play informed by the same sources might provide a startling dramatic departure from, and simultaneous *hommage* to, Shakespeare's creative decisions and his dramatic insistence upon consistent inconsistency.

So I had the outline of the story of the rival regents, Morgan and Cundah, and the question as to how Edgar, and the other characters left at the end of the Shakespeare play, Albany and Kent, might relate to them. Then two startling female characters appeared to me in separate dreams and insisted they were forces to be reckoned with. And a shadowy, distinctly un-English figure began prowling round my imaginings, watching and waiting for his cue to act decisively.

I gave him the name of a district of Luxembourg as I had resonantly misheard it from the mouth of a particularly Nietzschean friend: Echternacht.[x] The name suggested to me a German mercenary fighting with the French army, and therefore stranded in England as a prisoner at the end of Shakespeare's play; it also evoked the strange unpredictable poise of my Luxembourgish friend, Eric Schneider, who would, years later, incarnate the role onstage. I know from accounts of Kemp and Armin that there are good precedents for writing roles with the distinctive energies of unique performers in mind, if only initially. But perhaps my most Elizabethan achievement occurred when I was working on the second draft of the play: I caught the pox.

Chicken pox, to be precise, from my children. With little to do but fester and imagine, I feverishly developed for Echternacht a surreal hallucinatory odyssey parallel to that of Edgar in Shakespeare's play, a sidestep out from the main dimension of the play in order to equip him for a decisive re-entry into it. For, in a play preoccupied with the question of what might be on the other side - of every one and every thing - Edgar was my tragic hero, dislocated by his experiences on the heath from ready compliance with the postures of power, as he recounts whilst he completes Lear's abortive ritual gesture of self-disclosure:

> King of England? Where rules are the rule? Thanks, but no. In this country, the only thing created is PROCEDURE: dutiful repetition so as to satisfy the requirements of external perception. I have better things to do than perch on the edge of a pattern in dust (*Removes his shirt*). Much less try to sell it to others (*Pause*). I want to go back to breaking the beaks off nightingales and plunging into lakes. I want to dog the shade, and wind it tightly around me. Reasons are pretty, but they leak. The trick is, tasting what they leak. (*Kicks off boots. Checks soles. Then...discards trousers. Stands naked. Then:*) I could show 'em patterns. Like the night, three gipsy sisters took turns to stretch their skins over mine. I played the bucking rack and they arched their backs above me, spread themselves like starfish across a branch. They never pounced nor squeezed the same way twice: each one could always dig up a new lustre, make their mouths leave different teeth-marks, forge their bites anew to leave skeins of blood as different as each cobweb in the frost. I've seen the wind when it's sucked out bracken and spat it out so hard that it stuck into the bellies of clouds, and raked the hills. I watched snakes throttle the skins they've shed, 'cause they remind 'em of how their new scales have failed to be as different as they'd hoped. How can you tell when a man loves a woman? He stops fucking her friends. How can you tell when a woman loves a man? She lets herself be fucked by his friends so that he can watch. I've seen it happen, with my very own eyes. (BoB 2:1)

Michael Mangan has noted how Shakespeare's *King Lear* presents a kaleidoscope of images of Lear and Edgar, often generating more than one perspective on a character at any one time, 'But the difference between Lear and Edgar is that Edgar plays out his set of roles, if not from choice, then at least deliberately. Lear has no such deliberation. The different Lears that we see are not consciously assumed roles: they are the result of a personality undergoing collapse'.[xi] My play gradually closes the gap between Lear's and Edgar's experiences.

Edgar begins his play bitterly ironic towards the trappings and machinations of power, seeking to irritate his self-appointed superiors with a series of ostentatiously self-cancelling irrelevancies. He is arrested by the new prince regents, Morgan and

Cundah, then adopted as a regal-advisor-*cum*-fool. They ask him to guide them to the lair of a witch, who may assist the revival of their barely alive aunt, Cordella (I thought it an apt estrangement to return to the ur-play's rendering of her name and of Leir's). En route, they encounter a tavern scoundrel, Scarecroak (in some ways a meanly predatory version of Falstaff) and his abused and vicious daughter, Wrayburn. After a skirmish, they locate Wye, who agrees to help out of curiosity. Edgar conceives an appalling desire for Wye, whose characteristic and compulsive provocative interrogations propel him back to the world of action, though primarily to win her favour.

I adopted what I perceive as a Shakespearian five-act structure. This was important in its determinations of the broad canvas and formal rhythms of the play. It also invited the harrowing dissolution of some aspect of the psychic terrain of the play to conclude the Third Act. In this scene, Cordella is flung into prison alongside the grief-maddened Kent and the existentially brooding Echternacht. Morgan and Cundah have pressured Cordella towards abdication, as a statement of public deference to them, but she has refused; now Cundah drives her to suicidal despair by taunting her and Kent with the stuffed corpse of her father. In despair, she commands Kent to undo her recovery and terminate her life, conscious that, whilst his mistress survives and calls, he must not say no. The ensuing strangulation (directed with a deliberately Hitchcockian sense of difficulty in self-overcoming) is promptly followed by the discovery of the corpse's hideously stitched visage, and the reply to Kent's question 'What else remains?', with an 'ABRUPT MASSIVE SHATTERING EXPLOSION AND BLACK-OUT'.

However, the sense of shock with which this scene sent audience members into the interval was generated not only, I would venture, by the pain and horror of any component detail or action in this sequence, but also by its deliberately *Lear*-like desecration of even the vestigial hope and deserved relief which Shakespeare, his directors, or his audiences, may associate with the characters of Cordelia, Lear and Kent.

The second half of *The Back of Beyond* opens on a lighter note, as Edgar attempts to win Wye's respect by initiating a counter-revolution based on imaginative anarchy. He tries to popularize this in a market-place, and his audience gradually and comically move from scepticism into dionysia. Meanwhile, Kent has been recaptured, tortured and incorporated into Morgan and Cundah's strategies. Echternacht's escape from the prison takes him to a wilderness, where Wye provides him with a strange epiphany: Leir's corpse, briefly reanimated as a stumbling automaton, is presented as 'the shell of hope', in contrast to her own beguiling physical immediacy; she also conjures up a spectral family, whose domestic routine provides an image of death-in-life, and with whom Echternacht lodges for a while.

When Edgar's counter-revolution degenerates into a campaign to fuel his own vanity and bid for power, Wye transports Edgar into Fooltime, a realm of hellish ritual ostensibly presided over by the insane Kent, who is now in fact manipulated by Cundah. Kent greets Edgar with a disturbing vision of his status: 'Alas, Poor Tom! I know you by your serrated horns, your many noses, those lunatic eyes. You have come to take your place in our Parliament of Fools.' Edgar protest that Tom is 'past and-buried', but Kent insists that he acknowledge 'the fathomless atrocity of (his) true countenance', and berates him for persisting in 'this heresy of endings'. In a scene consciously influenced by the unleashings of the lunatics in *The Duchess of Malfi* and *Peer Gynt*, Edgar finds himself encircled and pawed by deranged myrmidons who claim the identities of folklore spectres once invoked by Poor Tom - Marwood, Maho, Obidicut and Flibbertigibbet - claiming him as 'Hoberdidance himselve, who danced and lost his tongue'. Under this pressure, Edgar replies, 'No, I'm Tom (*They laugh uproariously.*) Edgar, I mean I'm Edgar', inadvertently encouraging their insistence on his reversion to what they propose as an essential disintegration. This episode is a deliberately malignant dramatization of a Shakespearian preoccupation, 'the limits of language - the extent to which words are adequate to 'capture reality', and the way in which meaning' - and identity - 'continually slips away'.[xii] For Edgar, it also represents a literally nightmarish experience in which the imagination loses control over its own artifacts and creatures, which turn against their former master (an experience which is also visited upon Macbeth). At the climax of a black mass designed to raise the spirit of Leir's Fool, vengefully deified, Cundah breaks Edgar in body, mind and spirit. This is also a profoundly painful moment in its wider repercussions: the shattering of the resources of language and articulacy - and of all who would associate with, and put their faith in them, particularly artists and wordsmiths - by the culturally nihilistic necrophilic control which Cundah consciously represents. Wye regrets her complicity in this unexpected depth of cruelty. Even Morgan challenges Cundah's tactics and assumptions, and his boast to be afraid of 'nothing'; in reply, Cundah kills him.

In the family's deathly hovel, Echternacht's fever breaks. He emerges, willfully transforming himself: 'Right then, Witch. Here is what is on the other side of me. It's everything. Everything from which I can step away free. And now I am unpredictable, even to myself ...I no longer want to be a man. I split my very core with change, become the change and not the core.' This is, of course, crucially divergent from Edgar, who denied the lasting effects of his own performance upon his identity, though it is similarly strategically wilful. Echternacht insists on his own difference, and his determination and ability to make further difference through asocial action. I use the term *asocial* in Eugenio Barba's sense: divergence from a society predicated on injustice, in order to test and perhaps realize a personal potential concerned with each individual difference.[xiii]

In the final scene, Edgar is a crippled outcast, playing the self-stigmatized bitter fool with the ventriloquist dummy of Leir's corpse which he has found discarded on a hillock. He surveys the Heartbreak House which Britain has become under Cundah: a wasteland of power which would refute the possibilities of imagination. Wye reappears, as provocatively curious as ever. In an enraged response to her reprised question, 'What's on the other side of you?', he demands she conjure three trumpet blasts. The invocation and reanimation of this climactic motif from *The Book of Revelations* and *King Lear* is distinctly characterized by Edgar, as he psychically merges his last-ditch desperation with Wye's defiant insatiability in a joint effort of wills. The first trumpet summons up Cundah ('one: who thinks he is the worst'); the second 'is the call, that is never answered: 'For that is the call of hope. And now we are beyond it.'

And now the unknown can start. And that is what I summon. For that is all that's left: beyond the worst: beyond the hope; let's go. Beyond. (He presses his brow against WYE'S.) I demand THIRD TRUMPET! THIRD TRUMPET!! TTTHHHIIIRRRDDD TTTRRRUUUMMMPPPEEETTT!!!

(It sounds. The note is prolonged into (artificial) impossibility, and pulls new sounds into being alongside it. Shadows congeal into a figure: it is ECHTERNACHT.)

CUNDAH: And what are you?

ECHTERNACHT: I Nothing am. To you. And that is my quality. And that is my purpose. And I shall see what's inside you, now.

Echternacht opposes Cundah with the utterance: 'Let us admit the consequences.' These may be the most centrally purposeful words for my play, if one admits Brendan Kennelly's proposition that, at best, 'poetry captures *consequences*'[xiv] (and I would include poetic drama in that project), being 'the art of relentless questioning'[xv] which, 'by definition, is always breaking through boundaries and categories. To try to inhibit or limit that function is to do violence to the very nature of poetry, to make it the sweet, biddable, musical slave of our expectations'.[xvi]

Echternacht fights until Cundah is defeated. Edgar asks Wye to release him into death, preferring the exhaustion of a romantically tragic death to more life - 'No more work that I can do,' he tells her, 'so kill me and keep me yours forever.' Echternacht recognizes the volatility of his own moral state, 'answerable only to (him)self', and prepares to turn away from all society until his next inevitable transformation. However, he finds himself poised opposite the similarly lethal Wrayburn: *'they spring into each other, as to either kill or kiss or both.'*[xvii] Wye reflects on the rigours of change (in the opening words of this article), and walks away free.

The designer of *The Back of Beyond*, Russell Dean, identifies the play as Shakespearian in terms of its 'exploration of strategies for self-construction and annihilation' in which 'one will often masquerade as the other', and in which 'language is often a tool for release and imprisonment'.[xviii] His first instinct was to provide a partial release from this world of 'beguiling savagery', 'a place beyond the snares and limitations of words'; initially through the provision of a background of ragged drapes, 'in some ways representative of the skeptical sky over the action of the play' but more so as a delineation of 'Beyond', 'an ultimate escape into the unknown and as such the domain of Wye, the witch. This semi-opaque surround also provided that most Shakespearian of devices, the disclosure or discovery space, put to supernatural use as Wye's portal between worlds and places, quite literally at the lifting of the veil.' Within this veiled world Dean designed a structure 'inspired by the flinty expanse of Salisbury plain', specifically by the 'half-digested history' of the landscape, 'scarred with past civilizations' yet reclining and undulating 'beneath the kiss and lash of the skies': a broken circle of a wall was set at a tilt so as to appear to be either sinking into or rising from the surface of the stage, resembling 'a jagged broken tooth piercing the playing space, with actors stamping upon the cracked rim as dancing upon its exposed nerve'. This semicircular structure served to delineate space once again within the veil so as to conceive 'a space within a space within a "beyond"', the hard flinty surface of the wall apparently contrasting with the veil's tendency to disintegration, though this dichotomy was problematized as Wye produced various objects from within the wall by means of concealed traps and boxes.

Within this space, the performers employed various contraptions, principally designated as a wheelbarrow-table, a wheelchair and a torture device: rough, mobile and freely but deliberately constructed practical objects capable of sudden transformation and customization. For example, the torture device was a combination of rack and seesaw on wheels, capable of careering round the stage at the hands of the performers, trapping them and acting as the vehicles of their desires, as a 'visual and practical aid to the free-wheeling use of dialogue and metaphor'. Costume tended towards a twentieth-century eclecticism, often designating characters as 'recognizable types ready to be uprooted and raked by the storm', incorporating initially recognizable features to be transformed and destroyed: the cut of Echternacht's dark military costume suggesting the precision with which he dissected the world around him and suggesting his malcontent position; Morgan and Cundah first seen in matching public school uniforms, suggesting two sixth formers recalled to royal duties (Dean imagined 'Rosencrantz and Guildenstern combined with Lewis Carroll'). More outlandishly, Wrayburn combined a gauntlet claw with torn fishnet stockings and a thigh length dress, eliding adolescent 'bus shelter sexuality' with blades prepared to 'speak the unspeakable with a single twitch'. Standing apart from these twentieth-century types was Wye, who appeared as in the dream in which she announced herself to the dramatist: ambiguously provocative, with bare breasts, black-painted eyes and nipples, and elbow-length gloves. A waistcoat derived from that of a Minoan snake priestess further sculpted her torso whilst dramatizing both a stone/bone necklace and her exposed but redesignated breasts; 'Sex was undoubtedly part of her magic but only as a generator for other strategies; a means to an unknown end.'

The central playing hemisphere was initially sprinkled with sawdust, suggestive of the recurrent bear-baiting imagery in the play, but capable of being redrawn by Wye as an invocatory circle, then rapidly broken by her, to linger in imperfect form throughout subsequent action. During rehearsal, Russell Dean also led the company in a day of mask-making and workshop exploration, which yielded an expressive array of grotesque muslin and foam masks. These were used in the market-place scene, in which Edgar addresses passers-by with his theories of running the country, and overcame the problem of a small cast whose faces were all strongly associated with their main characters by the second half of the play, 'creating a de-individuated crowd and isolating the mask-less Edgar in one fell swoop'. This 'monstrous audience' took on a life of its own, with new, anarchic scenarios emerging from the performers' interactions in new identities, indeed suggesting performers' and characters' potential to go, in Wye's words, 'beyond the boundaries of the play in which they're placed'.

The spirit of my play, and the name of my theatre company, Lurking Truth/Gwir Sy'n Llechu, is perhaps best amplified by Jeanette Winterson's words in her novel, *Gut Symmetries*:

Is truth what we do not know?

What we know does not satisfy us. What we know constantly reveals itself as partial. What we know, generation by generation, is discarded into new knowings which in their turn slowly cease to interest us.

In the Torah, the Hebrew 'to know', often used in a sexual context, is not about facts but connections. Knowledge, not as accumulation but as charge and discharge. A release of energy from one site to another. Instead of a hoard of certainties, bug-collected, to make me feel secure, I can give up taxonomy and invite myself to the dance: the patterns, rhythms, multiplicities, paradoxes, shifts, currents, cross-currents, irregularities, irrationalities, geniuses, joints, pivots, worked over time, and through time, to find the lines of thought that still transmit.xix

And the most vital transmission is surprise. I first-drafted (in 1996) then directed (in 1998) a sequel to *The Back of Beyond* itself, entitled *The Battle of the Crows*, in which the surviving characters from the first play continue their discoveries. More of that another time; but I mention it because my curiosity and courage were licensed by the Shakespearian initiatives to develop interrogation of, and challenge affection for, Characters - particularly one's own - so masterfully manifested in the History Tetralogies.

So, having said all this, what do I mean by my coinage and application, in this context, of the term 'Shakespearian dramatist'? I mean it as an identification of a dramatist who attempts a deliberately startling and consciously interrogatory re-animation of some pre-existing story or play; who leapfrogs early twentieth-century prescriptions of naturalism and concomitant notions of social determinism, in order to present a drama which manifests a fully poetic, and consciously poeticized, range of the most visceral emotions; and who considers the potential consequences of their expression, through action, as the pragmatics of power. A dramatist who works not in a spirit of documentary realism or towards so-called 'contemporary immediacy' - the platitudinous jostling of familiar because commercially defined fashionable surfaces - but who rather attempts to expose the struggle for the soul (or unlived life) of a nation state through the invocation of its dream-life and the contradictory animations of its spectres, in a theatrical arena where historical determinism can be challenged by existentially transformative action, which manifests the force of resistance behind every attempted maintenance, the incompleteness of every prescription; and indeed the incompleteness of every thing: its potential for terrible and beautiful new life; the disclosure of a further vocabulary of being. As my lady says: 'So tell me: what's on theother side of you?'

It would be absurdly slavish to write plays which mimicked the style of this least slavish and most subversive of dramatists, seeking 'to write Shakespearian plays'. But 'being' a dramatist who operates in what I feel to be a Shakespearian seriousness and playfulness is another matter, and a properly difficult endeavour for a writer/director.[xx] As Russell Jackson characterizes British Shakespeare performance at the hinge of the millennium: 'On a good night, the audience may leave with the feeling that they have actively participated in something that engaged them directly, with a mind full of new arguments from old matter, and an appetite for more'.[xxi] The more of that effect, the better. And, 'Let us admit the consequences.'

Notes

1. Howard Barker, *Arguments for a Theatre* (Manchester: Manchester University Press, 3rd edition, 1977), p. 153.
2. Andy Cornforth & David Ian Rabey, 'Kissing Holes for the Bullets: Consciousness in Directing and Playing Barker's *Uncle Vanya*', in *Performing Arts International* 1999, Vol. 1, Part 4, pp. 25-45.
3. Barker, *Arguments for a Theatre*, p. 154.
4. Peter Holland, *English Shakespeares* (Cambridge: Cambridge University Press, 1997), p. 265.
5. Stephen Booth, *'King Lear', 'Macbeth', Indefinition and Tragedy* (New Haven and London: Yale University Press, 1983), p. 6.
6. Ibid., p. 11.
7. Ibid., pp. 13, 15 and 22.
8. Unpublished 1983 essay by Ron Callan (now a lecturer at University College, Dublin), quoted with his permission.
9. In a letter of 24 January 2000, responding to a first draft of this paper, Eric Schneider comments: 'It could also be argued that what makes Shakespeare's theatre so inspiringly artificial is his complete disregard for psychological conventions. Whether a character, say Edgar, feigns madness, or is indeed mad, makes little difference; it has no bearing on the actual perception of madness. What is witnessed, must be true. Which explains why Edgar so often reminds us that actually he is not mad.'
10. The town's actual name is Echternach, and it also commemorates displacement: its monastery testifies to the efforts and Celtic influences of an expatriate monk from Lindisfarne.
11. Michael Mangan, *A Preface to Shakespeare's Tragedies* (London & New York: Longman, 1991), p. 177.
12. Ibid., p. 40.
13. See Eugenio Barba, *Beyond the Floating Islands* (New York: PAJ Press, 1986), pp. 209-12.
14. Brendan Kennelly, *Journey into Joy: Selected Prose* (Newcastle: Bloodaxe, 1994),p. 30.
15. Ibid., p. 36.
16. Ibid., p. 44. After writing *The Back of Beyond*, I learnt that my surname originally means 's/he who lives at or on the boundary'. This was detailed in a family history entitled *The Boundary and Beyond*, ed. Graham Peter Rabey (Fakenham: The Raby Family History Society, 1995). I was encouraged by both discoveries.
17. Schneider (see n. 9) comments: 'Wrayburn is probably the character who is most difficult to situate in the play, but also the one to challenge most the company producing the play. She is central to the play, yet defies description and analysis. Perhaps a short evaluation of what she means to you and to the play may enlighten

why she is the one to confront Echternacht and would bring this fascinating character a little out of the shadows, if only to disappear into the dark again.' However, and perhaps significantly, I find myself unable to provide this, and think the task better left to another.

18. All quotations from Russell Dean are drawn from a letter to the author, July 2000, for which I am, as for his other contributions to the production, very grateful.
19. Jeanette Winterson, *Gut Symmetries* (London: Granta, 1997), pp. 82-3.
20. This distinction is inspired by that of David Rudkin, 'Being an Artaudian Dramatist', collected as part of the Conference Papers of *Past Masters: Antonin Artaud Conference 8-10 November 1996* (Aberystwyth: Centre for Performance Research, 1996).
21. Russell Jackson, in *Shakespeare: An Illustrated Stage History*, ed. Jonathan Bate and Russell Jackson (Oxford: Oxford University Press, 1996), p. 230.

The Back of Beyond was first performed by the Lurking Truth/Gwir sy'n Llechu Theatre Company 27-29 April 1996, Theatr Y Castell, Aberystwyth, and at Cardiff Chapter Arts Centre 2 May 1996, with the following cast:

EDGAR - Roger Owen
LEIR - Mat Proe
CORDELLA/KILLICOE/MOTHER - Helen Longworth
ALBANY/DORRIDGE - Rob Storr
KENT/PHILPOT - Steve Schnell
BRIMER/FATHER - Gareth Smith
CUNDAH/VAGRANT - Alan Smith
MORGAN - Andy Cornforth
ECHTERNACHT - Eric Schneider
WRAYBURN - Claire Houlding
SCARECROAK - Richard Downing
WYE - Charmian Savill*
BOY - Gemma Allen/Katie Schreiber
Other roles played by members of the company

(* Hannah Oakey was due to perform the role of Wye, until she incurred an injury an hour before the first scheduled performance on 26 April. Charmian Savill immediately undertook the role to permit the production to open on 27 April.)

Director - David Ian Rabey
Original Music - Paula Gardiner
Designer/Maker - Russell Dean
DSM - Gemma Allen
Lighting Design - Julie Derevycka

The play then had its second production by the Lurking Truth/Gwir sy'n Llechu Theatre Company, in a revised version (the 'Back with a Vengeance/Ni Yma o Hyd' remix) which provides this published form, at Theatr y Castell, Aberystwyth, 4-6 October 1996, with the following cast:

EDGAR - Roger Owen
LEIR - Paul Higgins
CORDELLA/KILLICOE/MOTHER - Sally Bartholomew-Biggs
ALBANY/DORRIDGE - Stewart Monkhouse
KENT/PHILPOT - Steve Schnell
BRIMER/FATHER - Gareth Smith
CUNDAH/VAGRANT - Andy Cornforth
MORGAN - Alan Maddrell
ECHTERNACHT - Eric Schneider
WRAYBURN - Hannah Lavan
SCARECROAK - Richard Downing

WYE - Hannah Oakey
BOY - Heidi Sullivan
Other roles played by members of the company

Director - David Ian Rabey
Original Music - Paula Gardiner
Designer/Maker - Russell Dean
DSM - Heidi Sullivan
Lighting Design - Julie Derevycka and Jenny Quayle

Prologue

(*Into blackness: tight spot or bullet-beam onto face of EDGAR.*)

EDGAR: The oldest hath borne most: we that are young
Shall never see so much, nor live so long.
UNLESS

ACT ONE, SCENE ONE

(*Immediate snap to wash of white light, pricklingly cold. EDGAR kneels surrounded by
ALBANY, KENT, TWO CAPTAINS [BRIMER and ECHTERNACHT]. Prone: LEIR,
CORDELLA. On a breath, EDGAR hops up.*)

EDGAR: I decide not to be a dancing prince of dumbness. ENGLAND: land of wheezing hiatus, to be distinguished from its neighbours by its force of belief in yesterday or tomorrow, but never in today. The itch: to break its stride. Or let it break your own. ONCE UPON A TIME -

ALBANY: I think this may be a time to pause, for reflection.

EDGAR: To reflect what, exactly?

ALBANY: We must consider how to address the issues.

EDGAR: I AM ADDRESSING THE ISSUES. Each little issue, the swirl of juices out through my skin, the spitting of pictures out through the GRID of what I know, each one is meticulously and poisoningly franked: ENGLAND: nation cowardly in both its idealism and its cynicism. But then, I expect you are all doing the same, but if you aren't, then spare me the reason why not.

KENT: Let's tidy up.

EDGAR: Let's not.

ALBANY: Do you propose to leave the bodies to rot?

EDGAR: They'll rot anyway.

ALBANY: WE ALL KNOW THAT. STOP YOUR CONDESCENSION, YOU DOOM-BUOYANT SCAVENGER.

KENT: Please, this should all be elsewhere. All this: should be elsewhere. This French mutton (*indicates A CAPTAIN*). I myself. Or things could get stuck. And spread.

(*CORDELLA quivers*)

ALBANY: She quivered. NOW SEE WHAT YOU'VE DONE. WHERE WILL THIS END?

again – the fiddle – Geo Shutrai.

EDGAR: Once upon a time, the live and the dead proved too CONVENIENT. A princess decreed the introduction of a third category, the UNDEAD, for added vim and spice, and set the fashion herself, with typical generosity.

KENT: Oh no. I'm not having this.

ALBANY: Quick! A stretcher!

EDGAR: Come to think of it, a typically capricious manoeuvre by a notoriously playful little minx. The insistence of her mischief knows no bounds.

KENT: HOW CAN SHE DO THIS TO ME

BRIMER: SHUT UP. Did you lot never hear the saying, 'Better late than never'? Stretcher party, hurry. Signs of life here. (*BEARERS enter. They carry her away.*) Quickly, but carefully. The fate of an empire may depend on it. (*Turning to EDGAR, ALBANY AND KENT.*) Gentlemen: I request that you remain composed for the immediate period, which may prove crucial. I will be supervising your arrest. (*The word tolls in them.*)

ALBANY: At whose decree?

BRIMER: (*Producing a sword.*) AT MY DECREE. My lords, shall we adjourn to your temporary quarters? (*He ushers them off.*) You too, you French git (*To ECHTERNACHT*).

ECHTERNACHT: Actually, I am German. Though today, I fought with the French.

BRIMER: You'll sing the same words when we play the whipsong.

(*They exit. Enter, from back, MORGAN and CUNDAH*)

MORGAN: Cundah.

Hannah Lavan (Wrayburn), Alan Maddrell (Morgan), Andy Cornforth (Cundah), The Back of Beyond. *Photo: Keith Morris.*

CUNDAH: Yes, Morgan.

MORGAN: Today, in a way, we are made brothers.

CUNDAH: No. Today, in a way, we are made orphans.

MORGAN: It seems that my mother poisoned your mother. (*Substantial pause.*) Sorry.

CUNDAH: It seems that your mother then stabbed herself to death. Remarkable determination. But not much imagination. And what could you do about it?

MORGAN: But we have to make something out of our sorrow. Our loss. How will we do it, do you think? Differently, I suppose. I am afraid to think how differently.

CUNDAH: From now on, I have no reason to do anything except what I believe is right.

MORGAN: And our grandfather. Everything has killed him.

CUNDAH: No, Morgan. We did not kill him. Our mothers did not kill him. Who killed him?

MORGAN: Who killed him?

CUNDAH: SHE KILLED HIM. (*Pause. He scavenges LEIR's watch.*) Let's have him stuffed.

MORGAN: What?

CUNDAH: Stuffed, you know. The empty skin, packed up.

MORGAN: Sometimes I wonder about you.

CUNDAH: What?

MORGAN: You're suggesting we have our granddad stuffed?

CUNDAH: It's a reasonable proposition. If I were suggesting we stuff your mother, or even mine, I could imagine grounds for alarm.

MORGAN: Who do we command, anymore?

Roger Owen (Edgar): End of the Scarecrow speech, The Back of Beyond.
Photo: Keith Morris.

CUNDAH: Anyone who'll listen.

(*Wolf-whistle from offstage. Then, enter WRAYBURN, with a knife.*)

WRAYBURN: Right. If you don't give me money in three seconds, I'm cutting off one
                 of my fingers. If you haven't coughed up by two seconds after that, I'll
                 force you to eat it. And I doubt whether you'll feel like fucking me
                 after that. Time's up.

(*SNAP BLACKOUT.*)

SCENE TWO

(*Body length spotlight into darkness. EDGAR enters it.*)

EDGAR: King of England? Where rules are the rule? Thanks, but no. In this
                 country, the only thing created is PROCEDURE: dutiful repetition so as
                 to satisfy the requirements of external perception. I have better things
                 to do than perch on the edge of a pattern in dust (*Removes his shirt*).
                 Much less try to sell it to others (*Pause*).
                 I want to go back to breaking the beaks off nightingales, and plunging
                 into lakes. I want to dog the shade, and wind it tight around me.
                 Reasons are pretty, but they leak. The trick is, tasting what they leak.
                 (*Kicks off boots.*) So there I was, cleaving to a thicket, and this scarecrow
                 waddles up. 'And what did they crucify YOU for?' he asks. 'Moving
                 like a rook', says I. 'Turn it in', He says, 'you couldn't swirl a muddy
                 puddle. Me, I wanted to be left alone with a drink, then someone
                 asked me 'Do you have a mother, son?' I said yes, so they took a blade
                 and scraped my face off. Then they snapped my head clean off my
                 shoulders, and jammed a turnip on the point of my spine. 'Go home
                 and show her that, then', they laughed. When I started for the door,
                 they caught me, and nailed my arms across this line prop. Then they
                 tipped me over, snipped my cock off and said 'Use THAT for a nose'. I
                 stumbled outside to find the dark, but their laughter was strapped
                 onto me, like phosphorescent leeches. I been trampin' these woods
                 since last September, and came across my mother's hut some three
                 times by accident, but then all I could do was march and patter round
                 it after dusk. Anyone sees someone with a turnip for a head and a
                 pizzle for a nose, they're apt to be alarmed, how'm I goin' to explain it
                 to me own mother?' 'You could tell 'er it's the new fashion', I told him.
                 (*Discards trousers. Stands naked. Then:*)I could show 'em patterns. Like
                 the night, three gypsy sisters took turns to stretch their skins over
                 mine. I played the bucking rack and they arched their backs above me,

*Meanderity +
puar?*

spread themselves like starfish across a branch. They never pounced nor squeezed the same way twice: each one could always dig up a new lustre, make their mouths leave different teeth-marks, forge their bites anew to leave skeins of blood as different as each cobweb in the frost. I've seen the wind when it's sucked out bracken and spat it out so hard that it stuck into the bellies of clouds, and raked the hills. I watched snakes throttle the skins they've shed, 'cause they remind 'em of how their new scales have failed to be as different as they'd hoped. How can you tell when a man loves a woman? He stops fucking her friends. How can you tell when a woman loves a man? She lets herself be fucked by his friends so that he can watch. I've seen it happen, with my very own eyes.

a meeting - not elting?

(*He steps out of the spot. It is vacant for a beat, then lights up to general state. Indoors: EDGAR at the end of a bench also occupied by ALBANY, KENT and ECHTERNACHT. BRIMER stands.*)

conversation the action -

BRIMER: (*To audience.*) You can tell when somebody feels they are born to *an*
power. They stand around describing themselves. And this is often *generous*
merely an attempt to drum up interest in the moment when they take their clothes off. (*To EDGAR.*) But I warn you: if you remind too many people that you can be as much of a prat as anyone else, this may backfire. Not forgetting that nobody's going to take orders from someone whose cock is evidently smaller than their own. I can't believe I'm being so helpful to you in pointing this out. I'm at a loss to know why, luckily for you.

EDGAR: I feel better like this. Just turn me out, and you'll never see me again. Quick red mud and a dead tree and I'll flow away.

BRIMER: As it is, you're reminding people, well me anyway, of good mates, gorgeous women and grinning kids who ended up as hollow slabs of cold white lard. (*Throws a cloth.*) Cover yourself.

ALBANY: Do as he says. Try to scrape together some dignity.

he move real - naked a hell

EDGAR: Dignity, by which YOU mean the habit of ignorance. I'm tired of duelling clothes. Mind you, he reminds me of an even worse danger, which is the terrible energy of men who think themselves unattractive.

BRIMER: (*Rounding on him.*) I also watched my commanding officer cut down by you, Jack Lilybollocks. And now we have a sudden lack of royalty. Just when we thought we'd settled down old Leir by gently insisting that he was barmy, the princesses go doolally with poison and daggers. Is it

23

the inbreeding, do you think? And now, the Francfucker's back, but fluttering around the options of breathing or not, and her plumed broomsticks like MONSIEUR here (*indicates ECHTERNACHT.*) can't smell their cologne for their own runny bowels, when they can stand up at all that is. That leaves me with you three: an old loony (*KENT*), a young loony (*EDGAR*) and a boring loony (*ALBANY*). Plus two prince regents who haven't yet found out what they use, let alone where to stick it.

KENT: It's as I prophecied. Everything is spreading.

ALBANY: Shut up before they decide to spread you. (*Pause.*) Who do you mean BORING? (*A door slams.*)

BRIMER: The prince regents. Snap to attention, you flotsam.

(*They do, in their fashions. Enter MORGAN and CUNDAH.*)

MORGAN: Captain: the physicians cannot sustain our aunt. The question for us is: how hard to let them try?

CUNDAH: More to the point: what function might she serve? I have my own answer: to let me watch her twirl a while before she cracks. But this moment, like any other, casts two shadows.

MORGAN: In fact, we were weary to the point of sickness with being told that we are some way short of the traditional age of accession.

ALBANY: Well, after all, son...

CUNDAH: Who made the tradition? Who made the CLOCKS? (*Toying with LEIR's watch.*)

MORGAN: However: our counsellors warn us that Cordella, as surviving daughter of our grandfather, might prove a rallying point for some popular preference. This may be true, for all we know.

ALBANY: For all you know - ? Wait a minute. Who are these 'counsellors'?

EDGAR: Your highnesses: invent new grace, or go catsplitting, as your own impulses prevail. But might I briefly offer the lesson of a lifetime? Don't go chasing after, or away from, popular preference. Particularly when this popular preference is being defined by somebody older, less resourceful and in fear for their pension.

BRIMER: Who asked you to speak?

EDGAR: I DID. Your highnesses, how well do you know Captain Brimer? He is a virgin, but holds on to the excuse of having a good job. You can live like that in the gaps, but it's a mocking way to die, which I expect he will soon, if you look you can already see the damage in his face, which his superiors tell him is character. Assuredly it is. Or not.

ALBANY: Have you really lost your sanity?

EDGAR: Yes, deliberately, I chucked it away because it was making me a POODLE OF DOOM like you. Your GODLESS WOBBLES are a monotonous way of telling everybody to do nothing as persistently as you do.

ALBANY: (*Quiet, bitter.*) For someone who's thrown off his duelling suit, you show a compulsion to cockfight.

KENT: The time for the Parliament of Fools is drawing near.

BRIMER: What's that supposed to mean?

CUNDAH: Old maps are torn. I think we need a new counsellor, and a new tutor. (*Indicates EDGAR to MORGAN.*) He talks the best.

MORGAN: I don't trust him.

CUNDAH: Neither do I. That makes him interesting.

MORGAN: What sly part did he play in our mothers' death? Blood should be answered before all else.

ALBANY: Yes, but Morgan...

CUNDAH: No doubt it will be. But it's rarely when or how you expect. (*Indicates EDGAR.*) He's been out into the kingdom. He could be our weathercock. (*Amused.*) A weathercock of waste.

MORGAN: What about our broken auntie?

KENT: Oh let her die! Don't make her a mockery. She deserves to flee the earth.

CUNDAH: He talks like a bishop. (*To KENT.*) You can help build the church!

MORGAN: Reluctantly, the doctors are admitting more problems than they can deal with. They make abashed mutters about consulting The Hex. But they do not know where she's to be found. (*To EDGAR.*) Do you?

EDGAR: (*Pause.*) Two villages away. Or more.

MORGAN: They say she claims tribute: in the old style. Is this true?

CUNDAH: What matter? Let's set out, and taste our country. In new clothes and new titles. I've been thinking. I'd like to be Prince of Wales. And Cornwall. And you could be Prince of Albany.

ALBANY: Now wait. Wait because - because you're right. Yes. I'm beginning to see it now. This isn't revolution, is it? No. Morgan would never do a thing like that, would you, lad? No, this is - evolution. (*To others.*) He's doing this because he has to. It's the way of things. And I must help him. No wonder I felt a bit out of touch. It's because I am. It's obsolescence. It's where we all go. I must embrace it, like a - a haven.

EDGAR: You can't EMBRACE a HAVEN.

ALBANY: YOU KNOW NOTHING. You are not a FATHER.

MORGAN: Dad, Cundah and I have been talking and I think he's right.

CUNDAH: And to see The Hex, we need a tribute. A sacrifice.

ALBANY: Yes, of course you do.

MORGAN: So we wonder if, under the circumstances, you wouldn't mind.

CUNDAH: Thanks.

MORGAN: The sooner the better, I think. So your mind doesn't dwell on it.

ALBANY: Of course. I was about to say the same.

CUNDAH: (*Giving BRIMER'S sword to MORGAN.*) I think Morgan should help you. It's only right. And I should watch. To make sure.

ALBANY: Yes. I'll be glad to be of help. Even now. Not much more use left in this old head. Best a man can hope for, the chance to help the future along. I preferred the past. I thought I could do things. But now I'm just slowing things down.

26

CUNDAH: Yes. Could we speed them up a bit, please?

MORGAN: Cundah. This is a difficult moment for me and Dad.

CUNDAH: Naturally. Sorry (*Echoing MORGAN earlier.*).

ALBANY: Don't you worry, son. I'll do what I can, like I always did. I could use a rest.
I'll be glad to help. This isn't goodbye, after all. We'll see each other again. On the other side of everything. (*Pause.*) Or, if we don't, you'll always think of me, anyway.
(*Pause.*) You'll tell your kids - (*A chasm opens in him.*) No. You won't.
SOMEBODY SAY SOMETHING
SOMEBODY SAY SOMETHING
IF I'M DYING I WANT TO KNOW WHY

EDGAR: (*To ALBANY.*) You sad porridge. You have lost your name.

(*SNAP BLACKOUT.*)

ACT TWO, SCENE ONE

(*The Wilds of England: crazy, lurching music. Interlude: WRAYBURN rampant and defiant. Then her strength seems to shrivel at the entrance of PHILPOT and KILLICO with SCARECROAK, who snaps awake balefully. Bleed up smoky light of an alehouse snug on figures cramped around a table.*)

SCARECROAK: Humbled in demeanour: but ennobled in calling. I, Scarecroak The Unseemly, call to a head this convocation of sliding partners who constitute the ranks of the Tasty Old Wounds, by reciting, as none can but I, Scarecroak's Rules of the Snug.

    1. No admittance to the man whose hand does not shake. He will draw only the straightest lines between points, and thereby pare our time.

    2. Time is never called or considered, being so much snapped elastics in the girdles of love and hate.

    3. Hate can be chewed, but only spat into the receptacles that the gods choose to provide on that given night.

    4. Night will provide new ways of crawling, and various pitches of ink

with which to sign bonds. Respect its limitless invention, and emulate its resources in your eyes.

5. Eyes, when unfocussed, should be trained on wall and floors to maintain good fellowship.

6. Goodness resides in the plenitude of a glass, a silence and a grudge.

7. Learn the grace and the inevitability of the sliding of all things.

8. Beauty emulates the horizon, its stretch and ever-imminent promise.

9. Believe everything, since each certainty contains its contrary at its core. Ale sharpens the sight.

10. Slander only the dead, since all else will eventually enter our portal; trust in the ease by which all things and persons return, and thirst to level them on their arrival.

(*PHILPOT & KILLICO have grunted, muttered and chortled in assent throughout this familiar recitation, and conclude it with wheezy uproar and the raising of glasses. WRAYBURN approaches him sardonically.*)

WRAYBURN: The landlord says you gotta clear the slate afore he'll let you 'ave any more.

SCARECROAK: Then he is a lump of sour froth and phlegm, unworthy of our custom. Have you winked up anything tonight?

WRAYBURN: Just pity copper and scoff nickel. (*A knocking at the door.*)

PHILPOT & KILLICO: SPEAK THE PASSWORD.

SCARECROAK: Lads: I sense this is not the time of the night to be exclusive. Let us admit fresh spit, and weave strange parables from their fears.

(*WRAYBURN goes towards the door, but hears it unlocked. She hides. Into the gloom: BRIMER, MORGAN, CUNDAH, EDGAR in cloaks or coats.*)

MORGAN: Good evening, gentlemen. We're told you've a knowledge of this place's outskirts, which you'll spill for beer.

SCARECROAK: Indeed, sir. This is our domain: on which we gaze so long and hard we twist the world's reflection. Welcome back to you all.

BRIMER: We've never forced this den before.

SCARECROAK: But you have. If you fumble for a picture of the night, the ale has danked it down. Everyone loops up here, then strays away until the fine sad echo of their beckoning back. But I'll remind you: I am Captain Scarecroak, speaker in eminence for this unstraightened band of tankard devils, known by all as The Tasty Old Wounds. My fellows in depth: Philpot, and Killico (*They bow*). When the rooves turn white, we preside, from the fire.

PHILPOT: (*Grinning*.) The Captain, he's a terrible man. He'll make you eat your own tongue.

CUNDAH: We're looking for a witch. The landlord says you'll direct us to the lair of The Hex.

SCARECROAK: The Hex: oh yes. Brave foolish men, to try to see her. Be warned: she'll show you a face that'll strike blood across the land behind your mind. But let us entertain you first, with a different face: different to any thing. My dear hagspawn: Wrayburn. You see, gentlemen, her skin rendered up in defiance of me and the world. She pierces everything to get what she wants, then pierces that too. My scalding nightmare girl: if she can't make you pay to stop her slitting herself, she'll make you pay to try and stop her slitting you, which she usually does, anyway.

BRIMER: You threaten us? You taproom toads?

(*WRAYBURN has behind her back a gauntlet impregnated with long curled sharp hooks. When BRIMER glances to SCARECROAK she intervenes, arcs her claw down, and up. BRIMER shrieks to discover his nostrils slit.*)

SCARECROAK: Spliced yer nostrils, eh? That takes me back. I think she was eight when she first practiced that on herself 'cause she wanted the last knuckle of pork. Though as you can tell, she's been stitched and torn again a good few times since when she's had a spat with herself or her - elders. Shall we discuss terms, gentlemen?

BRIMER: HELP ME, SOMEONE. (*PHILPOT soaks a rag in a tankard and tosses it to BRIMER, who clasps it to his face to staunch the blood.*)

MORGAN: Cundah. It's the girl.

CUNDAH: Yes. (*To EDGAR.*) We've met before. She came up to us and chopped her finger off. I had to pay her to try and stop her force-feeding it to Morgan.

SCARECROAK: Is that so? Full of pranks like that, my little blood widgeon. She'll show you all, in turn.

EDGAR: No, now it's my turn. Full of pranks, eh, Wrayburn? Well, now's your chance. Think back to the first pain you can remember. Recall that tickling finger that first made your pink parts red, and the white knuckles that pounded you for enjoying it. Look for the face above, with its slack leathery grin curling into a snarl. Is the face here? It's not mine. Search out those eyes that pleaded like a dog then ground you down into the dirt. Who is it that still slangs you like a dolly to suck his pride and jerks you from the edge to scrape together the coins for his pap? Now's the time you could really cut deep, and show him you have more teeth than he can guess. So where is he, Wrayburn? Here?

WRAYBURN: (*Falters: with a laugh of sour spite.*) Yes. (*Points her claw at SCARECROAK.*) THERE.

EDGAR: Right. (*In the second she changes focus, he steps inside her claw hand and sends her flying with a blow. Pins her down and removes the gauntlet.*) So why should I let you breathe?

PHILPOT: Scarecroak, you poxy old cuntflap. You and your offal puppet have us straddling the blade.

KILLICO: Best tell 'em what they want, before you gall 'em worse.

SCARECROAK: (*Kilning his broken pride.*) Up the hill past the church. Past a burnt-out farm, through a copse to a dead lake. Other side: cliff dwelling, in the red sand wall. You can dig her up, and once you've pulled her out she'll scream you into the grave. Heh.

EDGAR: (*A moment of fixation: he breaks it.*) Your highnesses: help Captain Brimer to the air. (*They do.*)

BRIMER: The girl -

MORGAN: You'll meet your moment, Captain.

CUNDAH: So will you three cankers.

(*MORGAN and CUNDAH with BRIMER, then EDGAR - tossing down gauntlet disdainfully*

- leave.)

KILLICO: Once I was a squire. Then a woman changed me into a cat, that was hung on the bears at the baitings. She called me Lusty Jolly Jenkin and between the baits made me lap her into milk, even while I bled from the bear. She had no face, being called Anonymous. One day her cowl blew back, and when folk saw the front of her head they daggered her. I lived behind her painted window till the river burst its banks, then sailed out on the slops, but both halves of her came after me. I lay in a creek until I spread into the mud. I sucked up a frozen tramp and used his bones as struts to build this body. I killed another for his skin, and broke another for his clothes. I kept me old cat eyes, and made meself hair from the fur I'd chewed out with the bits of bears. I let the woman catch me, then stroked her with a hatchet I'd found in a ditch till I saw her lungs. When I ate 'em up, I swallowed her voice too, but one day if I tell this right I'll be able to shit it out and never have to talk again.

PHILPOT: Ay.

SCARECROAK: Ay.

KILLICO: (*Sigh of disappointed realization.*) But not this time.

SCARECROAK: Come on, let's pawn our jackets for another round, then strip the drunkards where they roll. Another drink, Killico, it'll help you try again.

KILLICO: It might feed the voice. But it might grease it out. (*As they exit:*) Once I was a squire. Then a woman changed me into a cat that was hung on the bears at the baitings...

(They leave. Wrayburn lifts her head and nurses bruising: then stretches out to find her gauntlet, and pulls it back onto her fist. Fast fade to black.)

SCENE TWO

(Into blackness: spot on WYE. She is bare-breasted, and her eyes and nipples are blackened. During this speech, she dons black elbow-length gloves, a necklace and perhaps a tunic that nevertheless leaves her breasts exposed.)

WYE: I tell those who require explanations: the reason I rub coal onto my nipples to show that I am not a pelican. To show that no one sucks life from me. I cook henbane and wormwood on the edge of the villages:

31

Albion's little clusters of disappointment. But I was too quick to be a hutfucker, so let the rest of them breed foppets. By 'foppet', I mean something that can't decide whether or not to strap its arms around a sluice of air or a back without asking their mothers beforehand. Once upon a time, there was a little girl whose daddy was a cinder, so she set out to find another daddy and make her fortune. On the way to the city, she met someone who wanted to be a real live boy, so she gave him a conscience which lived in his handkerchief. This made sure he never blew his nose nor waved goodbye. Until the conscience flew up his nose and turned him into a cricket, and he became immediately mesmerised by the sound of his own legs rubbing together. The little girl let him do so, until he also caught fire and burned down to a cinder.

For the right fee, I can take misfit hutfuckers up to the heights which they then believe they invented for themselves. They offered me a life as a face crushed beneath the surface of a frozen lake. I offered them release: the sort of release that always lies on the other side of a door marked 'Self-betrayal' (*Looks at self in mirror.*). But so do all ways of making money. Concocting delusions is no true challenge; nor was it my purpose through these years I've spent studying the arts of magic. (*Langorously but provocatively, her gloved finger traces the contours of one of her breasts*) I knew I wasn't cut out to be transparent; so I hit on the idea of letting them scratch a mirror, and then asking them how they liked their faces. (*Her finger strokes and excites her nipple.*) They feel my meaning on their skins. (*A knock at the door.*) Yes?

(*Sound of unlatching. A bloodstained sack is thrown in, to crack or roll. Pause.*)

Now, I'd say that's a head. Too hard to bounce, too fresh to burst. Well, the hutfuckers are livening up, nipping each other's faces off before they even step inside, perhaps they want the fun of watching me try to stick them back on. That's what Mirth has come to, in a land of defeated irony. ARE ALL THE STONES USED UP, THEN? After stones of rock, then stones of flesh, but let's have RIGID BROKEN IMPOSITION, or the catapults will sink to perished rubber.

(*Enter* MORGAN, CUNDAH.)

MORGAN: The Prince of Albany.

CUNDAH: Wales and Cornwall.

WYE: If you are so extensive, don't let me detain you, scoop up my hut and pop it down somewhere else more convenient to you. And take your

Hannah Oakey (Wye), The Back of Beyond.
Photo: Keith Morris.

dad (*indicates sack.*) along for the laugh.

(*Enter* EDGAR, *followed by* BRIMER.)

EDGAR   In fact - you're correct. The former Prince Albany.

WYE: Demanding job, then.

EDGAR: Persuaded to forgo his head, so as to moisten your favour. How many men have done as much? No truth like a dying gift.

WYE: If freely given.

EDGAR: We seek no less. We are come to implore your skills in healing. One of the royal party languishes, beyond our doctors' reach.

WYE: (*Seeing* BRIMER.) I don't do nosebleeds. Try the herbalist.

EDGAR: Not him. The Queen of France. The Princes' Aunt. A broken neck. But she breathes still.

WYE: (*Indicates sack.*) One broken neck to set another?

EDGAR: We'd heard of such steep fees, to fuel your distillations and your pleasures.

WYE: Archaic prattle. I take what you speak of as and when I wish.

MORGAN: We entreat.

CUNDAH: And insist.

WYE: (*A beat.*) Why not?

SCENE THREE

(*Into darkness, tight spot on* CORDELLA.)

CORDELLA: Hanging on, hanging between, hanging down. At the rim of the poorest hour, things take on an appalling freshness. I am twined around a contraption which coughs to burst its skin. I recall being alive: when the sun shone, I felt smaller than the land. When the rain fell, it nailed things in. I grew to like that, it reminded me of home.

34

Then the world broke, and the ground quaked, and threw things upside down. I plunged down through floors, past floors, beneath floors, jerked awake at this angling slippage. My eyes and tongue worked to scare away life itself, and I stretched and thinned my every inch to try and reach - what, I wonder? The back of beyond?

(*Beside her: WYE.*)

WYE: Up she goes, down she flows,
Time to hoist her downwards,
Swing the depth, rear through death,
Drag her up like a puppet on her nerve strings,
I've no care for swallowed air,
Spit it back and there's plenty who will breathe it,
Wrench and drench and quicken, wench,
Twitch and quatch and tumble through your eye-holes,
No rest here, sorry dear, scorch and sear and shoot into your next life,
Kiss your fear, pull it near, chew its leer till you wear its blood as lipstick,
Can't stop here, can't stop here,
WE HAV-EN'T FIN-ISHED YET.

CORDELLA: (*As if screaming herself awake.*) NO, NO, NO, NO, NO, NOOOO!

(*EDGAR is lit, apart from them and to one side.*)

EDGAR: Oh, yes, oh yes. Oh. Yes. Oh. You incandescent animal.

(*Light fades quickly on WYE & CORDELLA; light spreads on EDGAR, taking food to ECHTERNACHT & KENT, who are both manacled.*)

EDGAR: (*Boiling in displacement.*) Well, what better skill can a man behold in a woman than the power to raise the dead? I tell you two because you won't understand me, but if you do, it will make you appreciate the prospect of freedom even more, presuming you're ever offered it, of course. You see: your punishment spares you pain: the deep pain which splits you open when you behold a magnificent woman, and you suffer for her till your whole being flickers, and you dread to speak it and invite contempt: but you also dread to let it go unspoken, swelling up in your gut, bloated like a drunkard with your own contempt for yourself that you didn't choose to be the other men who you watch fluttering around her. The taunting truth that makes you both curse and thank the day her path crossed yours, because it's shown you the glory and sorrow that lay outside the limits of your

35

own imagination. And the pain that resides in your choice, to approach that promising damnation, or to let it pass. Now YOUR so-called punishment RELIEVES you of such precious pain, by sparing you such sights, and removing choice. DON'T WORRY. As luck would have it, I am subverting your deprivation by providing communion with my true suffering - no, please: spare me your cataclysms of gratitude - whilst assuring you that I suffer even more intensely, ALMOST AS IF on your behalf. It's almost comradely to be able to offer you my own stimulating dejection. It may also save you trying to digest the food. You see: you are not forgotten. Thank you.

(Pause. Without seeming substantially unburdened, KENT and ECHTERNACHT exchange glances of resignation and begin to eat, unenthusiastically. Light fades on them, and raises on CORDELLA, on a wheeled pallet, MORGAN, CUNDAH.)

MORGAN: As usual, auntie, you create problems, but Cundah and I read them differently. I believe that most people are like myself: they take pride in a sense of their own purpose, which is most fruitfully expressed in common reference to an agreed set of images. This purpose, and these images, are focussed in the form of law. To obey and further this law, through choice and will, is true courage, socially expressed. We need images to reflect us back heroically, at times when pride in citizen and community might seem to have shrunk to mere routine. Now, you might provide such an image, if I might suggest. Your renowned selflessness, persistence and integrity, and your blood-linear connections with our grandfather and now with our potential rival, France, present an impressive and inspiring set of qualities for the people to love and trust. However, you have yourself repeatedly voiced a disinclination to proceed in matters of governance of state.

CORDELLA: You expose my inclinations to settle for less. But I resent your implications that, therefore, I am shallow. I'm just tired.

MORGAN: (*Truly stung.*) I said nothing about your being shallow! On the contrary! You represent charity and inclusiveness -

CORDELLA: AND YOU REMIND ME HOW DIFFICULT I HAVE ALWAYS FOUND KINDNESS. In that, at least, our family were alike: myself, Ragan, Gonorill, our father. But I was the most exclusive, and spoke love with no concessions to the immaturity of others, their incessant loping and grating to smother their own insecurities inside other people's. I should have known: build a boundary, and you invite its broaching; but afterwards, build anew. Even a barren cell might hold a space of self-possession, and thus conduct love. I am exclusive, Morgan: I acknowledge difference. You find difference threatening to the superiority you have presumed. Speak to pride, if you want to command respect. But it's never the same in any two people. So spare me the immaturity of your kindness, which only seeks control, because you yourself are scared of what you might allow. I suspect this comes of a repeated failure in attracting women, by the way...

CUNDAH: Oh, but my cousin does admit difference. He admits that I am different from him. I obey no images: I make my own, or proceed without them, in the workings of my will. I think you're right, auntie; he is scared of what he might allow. It's me. I am what he might allow, but dare not. I think you and I have much more in common, don't you?

CORDELLA: You should know better than to attempt ingratiation with me, Cundah. But at least you do not seek to salve yourself with apology before the brutal act.

MORGAN: What is 'brutal' about asking you to express a formal preference that we rule? You can then retire to convalescence in France -

CORDELLA: It's that word, 'then'! It sweats brutality! I do what you want, and 'THEN' I might be permitted my will if, as, and when you decree! ONCE UPON A TIME, THERE WAS A KING WHO HAD THREE DAUGHTERS. DURING THE DAY, HE WAS A PELICAN KILLING HIMSELF TO FEED THEM; BUT ON THE NIGHT OF THE FULL MOON, HE OPENED THE FURNACE OF HIS WOLFISHNESS AND FED IT WITH HIS CHILDREN. Don't worry, I am used to being presented with proposals which I am not supposed to be able to deny. Eccentric ramblings of a prematurely senile cripple, pay no attention, I'm sure no one else will.

CUNDAH: Morgan. I think we'd better do it my way.

(*Fade to Black.*)

SCENE FOUR

(*EDGAR and WYE.*)

EDGAR: I have witnessed so much. From the rim or edge. But grasped little. I shy away. Until Tom. Even he. A depth of strategy. Which yielded - (*Pause*). To take the pitch of contempt, to work up and through the worst, and thus to be some thing. The reach of that: beyond shy

Edgar's dreams. I spied on burstings; felt a prickle: took care not to be blasted. Defied that foul fiend.

From chambermaids and waiting-women. To smell of blood and gypsy juice. Shadows, bursting into me. I long, through watching. Until you: I long to fathom. I want knowledge of you. I need to undo the larceny of your belt, merge with your skirt, dig for the smouldering nectar'd ramp of your cunt. I stand and lie in my need for you. I beseech you. Please, unclose.

WYE: Not the words of a naïve boy spectator. Not the sense of a man who sees me clearly. More the verbal grapplings of a man fascinated by his own potential for craftiness and careful frenzy.

EDGAR: (*Exasperated sigh.*) Perhaps. But no fear of you.

WYE: Yes, it's the flipside of veneration.

EDGAR: All right, fear, yes of course fear; what's the point of the unknown if it's safe?

WYE: The point of the unknown: is to be unknown.

EDGAR: Says the woman with the thinnest of veils on her nipples. Easily licked away, I'd imagine.

WYE: You imagine.

EDGAR: Yes, I - OH GOOD, AN ECHO CHAMBER FOR COMPANY. HOW INVIGORATING.

WYE: Your rightful domain, your low-highness.

EDGAR: Not any more. How should I prove it to you?

WYE: Why are you playing court jester to Morgan and Cundah? You will most likely be the first victim of your own lethal flippancy. Like any other governors, they can imagine nothing beyond institutionalised possessiveness. Oh, you have a wit for clever antics, even for sensual deception. But where is your strength for refusal? I live by my wits, and from three strategies: insist on ingratitude; reject reconciliation; refuse complicity in any thing. They've kept me alive this far.

EDGAR: And brought you here, inside the palace walls...?
WYE: Oh, next you'll be saying that money equals truth. Spare me the limp

twitches of satire; I don't find it erotically pitiful. I'm following my instincts for something that may serve my purpose, but I don't ask or expect to know what that purpose may be.

EDGAR: (*Considers a moment.*) Perhaps a dancing prince of dumbness after all. My stride broken.

WYE: To make true change, you have to cut deeper than surfaces. You must create gaps in creation.

EDGAR: Fine. I'll throw up after lunch.

WYE: Your humour is the sound of you grating against your own self-disgust.

EDGAR: Yes. I admit.

WYE: (*Raises her skirts.*) I admit.

EDGAR: (*He approaches, looks, stops:*) Why?

WYE: Wye. (*She guides his mouth to her crotch. Lights fade.*)

ACT THREE, SCENE ONE

(*Sound of wind. A heath. BRIMER enters.*)

BRIMER: Bull of a wind. Rancid moon. Well, I'm hammering back. Even winter can be stopped, I say. SHOW YERSELF! I'm not cold. She ripped my brains out through my nose, and now my head's a brazier, flaming so high I don't have to carry it anymore. Light enough, to dog you by. I saw Horror back there! I left it with the rest, flyblown dead in a ditch. But I sucked its pockets first.

(*Behind him, shadows of WRAYBURN, SCARECROAK in a wooden barrow, over which smashed legs dangle grotesquely, pushed by PHILPOT.*)

SCARECROAK: 'Tis but the first day of Winter, Captain; don't rush to get yer bones wet. The rain will find out your faults, and you'll spit them yellow from yer mouth like the rest of us.

BRIMER: Good. At the lair of the lags. Only the matter of time. (*Laughs.*) You a bucket-rider now, Scarecroak?

SCARECROAK: When the devil drives, boys. The new trick from the towns is smashing ankles for company, so they know the ones, who can walk still have some money or food, or some cunt or arse not riddled yet. Old Killico forfeited his feet, and we left the woman voice leaking out of him in cries. (*He steps out of the barrow. The smashed severed legs have been concealing his own still-workable ones.*) Luck's with us, that they look at Wrayburn's face and figure the rest of her's the same. And they don't usually try to ransack me, 'cos they can tell I'd probably enjoy it. I enjoy most things.

BRIMER: What else? What are people planning?

PHILPOT: Keeping their own families alive at the cost o' somebody else's. The harvests failed: the land's locked up, and so's the old king's thronegold. Morgan and Cundah are busied, squatting and squabbling over it like dogs. But no one's surprised anymore. Some say Cordella's carousing with them. Time's enclosing.

BRIMER: Yes: the regents see no further than their gates. And is this then the matter of the land? So soon, so shrivelled?

SCARECROAK: Beggary and madness spread from courtly fashion now. They say Kent's in prison, and Edgar's shut up inside the grilles of his own wits, since Albany was killed.

BRIMER: Well, here's one, Captain Brimer, 'll stake himself to this ground. (*WRAYBURN laughs. To her:*) And raise you up, my Duchess of dirt, once we've worked some business between us.

WRAYBURN: (*Hisses like a cat.*) Stay back, or I'll scotch your other nose.

BRIMER: Yes, I wear your stripes, and they brought me a strange freedom. First woman, since my mother, could make me change, and I see the printed truth of your touch in every mirror ever more. I'll grasp and wear the rest of you, too, and thus I'll master what you tore loose from me, you salt bitch.

SCARECROAK: And what would you give us for her, Captain, short of a daggering?

BRIMER: Royal patronage and pension, Scarecroak: could await us all. I say Kent's our cross and anchor, the people's patient hope. I'll spring him from his cage, with your help and sleight in thievery. But first, you're right, there's daggering to be done, and there's the wench I long to give a stab or two.

PHILPOT: Who giveth away this woman? (*To SCARECROAK.*) Captain?

SCARECROAK: Ay. From one captain to another. (*BRIMER goes to shake his hand on the deal. SCARECROAK tweaks his injured nose. He returns to the barrow and blows WRAYBURN a kiss. To PHILPOT:*) Forward!

(*PHILPOT pushes SCARECROAK off. Interlude: 'Domestic Arrangements'. A piece of physical choreography, developed from improvisation, which suggests WRAYBURN's subordination and sexual domination by BRIMER. In unshared but adjacent realities, their bodies do not literally touch, but WRAYBURN's anguish is intense.*)

SCENE TWO

(*In prison: ECHTERNACHT, KENT.*)

ECHTERNACHT: I have been trying to look beyond these irascible walls. First, I look back at where I have come from. I came out of people who were asking the question, what is a man? They did their best to make me into bits of their answers. Such as: judicious yet kind; careful but not remote; patient without being lazy; responsible, yet self-possessed; both loyal and self-sufficient. They taught me that I was shown, by what I commanded: money; men; land; women; animals; children; fear - fear in others, and in myself, of myself. They expressed confidence in me, not to succumb to what they glimpsed with their fear. Because you can trust a man who knows the limits of safety, a man who prefers continuity to risk. For that, he is prized.
When I look back: no one feels my absence as a lack. The continuity may even be smoother because of my absence, thanks to the substitution of my occasional erratic tendencies. My absence, like my presence, makes no difference. So I will not play the grieving exile.
So now: stymied times require the oil of invention.

KENT: WHEN ALL THE EVIDENCE CONCLUSIVELY INDICATES.

ECHTERNACHT: One can stew in a garden as well as liquate in a prison.

KENT: ORDER IS INSUFFICIENT AS A DEFENCE AGAINST WHAT CAN AND WILL HAPPEN.

ECHTERNACHT: The trick is to know the limits of what you know, and know when to step outside them.

KENT: THERE IS A WAY OF THINGS, INSCRUTABLE AND OPPOSED TO
THE HUMAN PERSPECTIVE. THE UNIVERSE IS MADE UP OF THE
ECHOES OF ITS JEERING. INSIDE THOSE ECHOES, WE LIVE AND
DIE.

ECHTERNACHT: On the eve of the battle, my corporal asked me, 'Why is life so
complicated?' I told him: 'Because idiots keep trying to make it so
simple.' But he died, of course.

KENT: ALL WE CAN DO IS LET THINGS SPREAD.

ECHTERNACHT: I must find a moment whose truth I can seize, use it to turn into
other things.

(*Sound of a cell door. Enter CORDELLA.*)

CORDELLA: Prison. So. (*Interminable pause.*)

VOICE OF CUNDAH: (*Echoing from above.*) Hello Cordella. Hello Kent. Hello foreign
thing. I thought you might run out of things to think about, or grieve
for. So I ordered a companion to be made up, ready for you.

(*A GAOLER enters, whistling 'God Save The King', pushing a figure in a wheelchair, covered
by a cloth. He leaves it with them; it faces upstage. After a moment, ECHTERNACHT whisks
away the cloth, disclosing the stuffed corpse of LEIR. KENT screams. CORDELLA glances,
then snaps her eyelids shut.*)

CORDELLA: (*Edging along the precipice that has opened in her mind.*)
Too late.
I've seen the face.
I have met the enemy.
The enemy is
all
that is left
of the one you
loved.

ECHTERNACHT: Was this - the King - ?

KENT: Oh my master. What is this new lesson you are straining to teach me?

CORDELLA: He is showing us - Kent - that there is no escape. We might have
suspected. Now we are forced to face it. Sorrow outlives the life it

42

mourns. The best we can do. (*She winds her own chains around her neck.*) Is to try and take it elsewhere. (*She pulls. Gasps.*) The cowardice of flesh. Hanging on to repetition as if it were hope. (*She pulls again. Gasps. Hoarsely:*) Kent. We command you. You must not say no.

KENT: Oh my mistress. I heed your call. (*He crosses to her, throttles her. It is a lengthy and strenuous process for them both.*) Lie still.

ECHTERNACHT: (*To corpse of LEIR, turning it away from the others, and to face the audience for the first time.*) Do you see what they have made you grin at? Perhaps Kent is right. That dimensions are lies. That faith is foolish.

KENT: (*Bewildered:*) What else remains? (*A challenge:*) WHAT ELSE REMAINS?

(*ABRUPT MASSIVE SHATTERING EXPLOSION AND BLACKOUT.*)

– INTERVAL –

ACT FOUR, SCENE ONE

(*Tight spot on EDGAR.*)

EDGAR: Out, from the labyrinth of love. Next, she says I must come into my own. Come into my own WHAT? Nevertheless: I can try. (*Lights up to general cover of a public square, with passers-by, and a secretary, DORRIDGE.*)
Listen. It falls to me to recreate England anew, once more. And you think: drivel. You see me and you think, he has eaten silly fungus. He wants to talk myth, which is comforting magical tales of how - rather than why - how you got to be as wretched as you are now, and how it's a jolly good thing too, when you look at it after having eaten enough of the silly fungus. Or else, you think, he wants to talk politics, in which case why listen to me or anyone else, because politics is the business of projecting your own limitations onto other people, eventually with a hatchet. Look: no hatchet. (*The passers-by say or suggest 'so what?'*)
So what, you say. Well, I am Edgar (*They do so again.*) I am the first and last of my kind, (*They do so again.*): and so is each one of you (*They pause*).
I propose that we make this country the imagined place, that we speculate in speculation itself, that we float the economy on lies. Dorridge, write this down. (*DORRIDGE flurries with a quill.*)
1: The only social structure will be generated by the financial encouragement of the most inventive lies. The assessment of these lies will of course require a central evaluation committee comprised of the land's most beguiling men and bewitching women, and I can offer my availability to commence the audition process at once.

1st WENCH: Oh yes, I've had that. 'Can't you trust someone for a moment? Just undress, lie on the ground, and do what I say'.

EDGAR: If you know of better ways to spend your time, I've no wish to detain you. 2: Lies will be evaluated according to their empowering effect. That is to say, he or she who most successfully rolls back the mothy grey carpet of what is deemed and sensed to be possible, will be rewarded for their effort, and regularly exhorted to outstrip even their own previous, wildest imaginings.

2nd WENCH: Go on, I wouldn't mind a go at outstripping yer. (*Laughter.*)

1st BLOKE: I'll outstrip 'im, with a strap an' razor.

44

EDGAR: 3: Nothing will be illegal, but repetition would go unrewarded, thus driving against the formation of habits, or any sense of an authoritative version of anything. The incessant re-creating of personal histories will inspire co-operative inventions of new futures, through play, not work. (*Murmur of intrigue.*)

2nd BLOKE: All well for you to say. How'm I goin' ter play the cattle into a barn?

EDGAR: You persuade people to help you, beguilingly. Everyone is invited to join in the search for whatever encourages citizens to listen to each other and assist, rather than obstruct, constructions of possibility on an upwardly sliding scale of outrageousness.

2nd BLOKE: How'm I goin' ter outrage the corn into growin'?

EDGAR: You give the most entertaining possible set of reasons why people should pay you more for the smaller amount you have, and they'll thank you gladly.

2nd BLOKE: No, I mean to eat, myself.

EDGAR: Persuade your neighbours how you would be the most enlivening and pleasantly surprising and amusing possible person for them to share their meal with. If they're thin in the pantry, join forces with 'em and extend the operation out to cover the whole parish.

1st BLOKE: I don't 'ave time too listen to fool's talk.

EDGAR: So two fools are better than one. One amuses your child, by impersonating a tit, or whatever, whilst the other keeps trying till he finds out whatever does makes you want to listen, or watch.

3rd BLOKE: 'Ere, bags I work with Molly.

3rd WENCH: Stump off, yer daft posset.

2nd WENCH: I'd 'elp you, Sam.

EDGAR: 4: A community of engaging liars, honing their and refining their seductiveness, will in effect achieve the perfect marriage of art and science. Schools of Philosophy, Fiction, Rhetoric, Imagery and Performance will take over from current form of education. All citizens will be resourced to attend until they develop their skills to a point demonstrably worthy of the more munificent independent existence of lying for a living. The schools will also consider illustration, musical composition and performance, as revered and noble sister arts. Also: cookery, winemaking, brewing and distilling.

3rd BLOKE: Don't sound bad.

1st WENCH: Ar.

EDGAR: 5: Pleasure and relief must likewise be formulated in terms which make no appeal to custom. The academics of the schools will pursue research projects in this direction during any time they are not teaching, or recovering.

2nd WENCH: Hey, we don't want them 'avin' all the enjoyment.

EDGAR: (*Laughs.*) Good, you're learning fast. You can join the teaching staff.
               6: We will go into business as capital global exporters of lies, our strategic offer to surrounding nations. Foreign citizens, hidebound by history books and shackled to their soil, will in time glimpse the appeal of our venture: the rulers will naturally resist, the citizens will naturally overthrow them, inspired by the most irresistible and successful form of imperialism ever imagined.

2nd BLOKE: You mean, like, lyin' contests with Ireland? Persuadin' 'em all to come over here...

3rd BLOKE: While they try to persuade us to go over there.

EDGAR: And you go, or stay, where the lies are most appealing.
               7: Clocks and calendars are abolished, but small hourglasses will be tolerated for cooking purposes. 13: -

3rd WENCH: 13?

EDGAR: All linear sequence is abolished. 9: Polite requests to undress and invitations to fuck will be received gracefully and considered seriously, but compliance or refusal will be at the discretion of the recipient. (*He restrains an excessive enthusiast.*). Their decision will be final, and greeted with proper respect. Renewed initiatives will be confined to those expressed through speech, writing, mime, dance or gaze. (*Whoops and cheers and prompt initiatives.*)
               11: I myself will supervise and assess the working of the fiction adjudicating committee, and make such regular changes in personnel as I deem fit. However, I confidently assure you that this will serve as

the most benign of regimes, being ordered, in so far as it is, by the kaleidoscopic riot of my own impulses, which so far, you will be delighted to learn, resist the stability which is intrinsic to tyranny. I ask only one tribute: that each citizen is asked to build their own effigy of me, in gratitude for my vision, on a daily basis. Prizes will be awarded on how substantially each said effigy differs from the previous efforts realized by the artist in question. Needless to say, no official version of my appearance will be circulated. (*DORRIDGE gives up & throws away his pen in overwhelmment. He merges with the throng, which is turning from panic to dionysia.*)

1st BLOKE: You'll never make it last.

3rd WENCH: But we can decide whether it does or not.

1st BLOKE: I can't think of a better idea. But when I do, you 'ave to listen to me.

3rd BLOKE: You 'ave to make me want to.

1st WENCH: Let's give it a try.

EDGAR: Oh yes. I AM COME INTO MY OWN. (*Blackout. Music.*)

SCENE TWO

(*The alehouse snug, again. BRIMER, KENT and ECHTERNACHT.*)

BRIMER: (*Passing tankards.*) Drink: warm yourselves. The dogged Earl of Kent: my guest. We are own masters now, to tackle the matter. Of England. I saw, when Morgan and Cundah sacked me for my striped face and two-edged talk, that we were kindred now, after all. We are banishing them, reclaiming the air itself with every breath that we go on to draw. And here's our German cousin, marooned by the failure of his adopted lord.

ECHTERNACHT: I am not complaining. I am a soldier of fortune and, because of that, a ruler's last priority. I have fought back through worse.

KENT: That prison. Was not a prison. It was a bush of revelation. I am unsundered, yet. My lodestone drags me on.

(*Enter SCARECROAK, WRAYBURN walking stiffly.*)

SCARECROAK: And we've dragged Philpot on, to an open ditch, and cast him with the other poor sour dregs. Triggering your blast powder blew him half away, till he could only matter half words: 'old. ack. gah. ligga. dlam'. We took it as a prayer, and tossed him out to ease beneath the surface. Old smashed sapling.

WRAYBURN: You knew the blast would take him apart.

BRIMER: I knew it might. Considered risk. Least vital wing of our forces.

KENT: (*Seeing WRAYBURN.*) Oh ho. Did you raze your likeness for a Master, too?

WRAYBURN: (*Bitter, wry snort.*) I am sick with masters. My new one here (*Nods at BRIMER.*) has punched my cunt so it hangs out like a tongue. Then he bids me call him 'master', and he laughs.

KENT: And will you handle the land alike, Brimer?

BRIMER: I am but learning on her, my lord. What harshnesses force fruit. She is - an education for me. I want to reach into this land with love.

SCARECROAK: What you want, what it costs. I'm wearied of it all, Give me ALE! To drown all calculation and forbearance! (*Drinks.*) And with enough, we'll drown old Death himself.

KENT: It is in vain: you cannot.

BRIMER: Tell him, Kent. At this turn in time, you alone can legislate. Your service was ever true.

KENT: Not true enough yet.

SCARECROAK: All this prattle smacks of rigour. Drink, and turn your tongues till they unsay all they have said, and then there's no more cause of grievance. Scarecroak's law. (*Belches.*) What we need is a hearty song, to push back the dank of the night.
(*Sings:*)　　When creditors eat hail for pepper.
The weathercock's the one high-stepper
And you're woken up by a lusty leper
Then toss your cap and bellow back,
AROOOH! There's freedom in each loss.
When crumpled kites fall out the skies
The landlord's taken both your eyes

The witch turns up to claim her prize
Then clench your thighs and bellow back,

(*BRIMER strikes him brutally.*) URKKK!

BRIMER: I'm growing tired of you, father-in-law. You don't sing true melodies. Befoul your way.

SCARECROAK: (*Wheezing.*) I'm - touched - by your gratitude, m'boy -

WRAYBURN: (*Laughing.*) Enough freedom there for you? Stay here, he'll show you more.

KENT: Domestic arrangements. This is what they always come down to. (*To ECHTERNACHT.*) You have a cleaner life.

BRIMER: You'll share our board, Kent. Tell me what you saw, and we'll think of what to do. And you can join us, German.

ECHTERNACHT: No thank you. I have decided to walk out of the door as if I know where I am going, and to laugh as loudly as I can. (*He does so.*)

BRIMER: What strange action. I cannot understand that man. Greet our guest, wife.

WRAYBURN: May you live to feel dogs crap in your broken skull.

KENT: I think I do. What else can you foresee?

WRAYBURN: My husband broken in his proudest hope. But I haven't found it out yet. I know it's not me, that's why I've kept myself alive.

BRIMER: She plots to confound me. But a soldier knows, that everything plots to confound him, he has to second-guess it quicker.

(*CUNDAH and MORGAN appear; they surprise and pinion BRIMER.*)

CUNDAH: Brimer: you poor

MORGAN: soldier. So predictable in your lodgings,

CUNDAH: and your company.

MORGAN: But you've given us an idea.

CUNDAH: We think I was right.

MORGAN: That Kent should head the church.

CUNDAH: We have decided to make him Archbishop.

MORGAN & CUNDAH: And you can all take part in his investiture.

(Lights fade as MORGAN ushers off BRIMER and SCARECROAK brusquely. WRAYBURN laughs in terrible abandon. CUNDAH assists, but stays behind with KENT. An interlude, 'The Interrogation', developed from improvisation, in which CUNDAH controls KENT by vocal sound and movement, working him through pain and crying to a final splintering into mad laughter.)

SCENE THREE

(In the wilderness: ECHTERNACHT.)

ECHTERNACHT: Hello, metallic purple sky. Hello, sandwich I forgot to pack. Hello, rotted dripping frontiers. Even fever can be an asset to the resourceful. It provides more opportunities for conversation. The sun, for example: I can hear it saying that I am only severed bait, left making mouths at the absolute stretch of INDIFFERENCE. And I can taunt it back: if you're so clever, what's behind YOU? *(Enter a VAGRANT.)* You know full well what I am doing: stalking the last ditch, to see what will try to claim me, and discover how we might entertain and refute each other. *(Sees VAGRANT.)* Swift unbidden delivery!

VAGRANT: Give, or I'll take.

ECHTERNACHT: I have no money. Nor food. And the clothing's past its heyday. But we could swap time.

VAGRANT: Oh fuck, an evangelist! I have piss for fortune. You can go, I'll waylay others.

ECHTERNACHT: *(Grabs him.)* No, you've started. Give, or I'll take.

VAGRANT: Do I look fortunate? HEY, THAT'S NOT JACKET, THAT'S SKIN.

ECHTERNACHT: Skin and more skin. My face is splitting its stitches in this sun, but then it's about time. I'll tell you things.

VAGRANT: No thanks.

ECHTERNACHT: No option. I too have sought the flow of money, the brief sweet indeterminacy of the unspent coin. It led me away from all I knew, which is its greatest benefit. But it can't see beyond its own patterns. The order it brings refers only to itself. This makes it poor company. It never fulfils its promise, and so drowns real decision. It makes you as free as a man whose destiny it is to be called JUDAS. Let us seek a deeper exchange.

VAGRANT: HE-LP! NUTTER GOT ME!

ECHTERNACHT: Oh, shut up, who would want to help you? You are utterly devoid of attraction or interest, and so a good place to start.

VAGRANT: I'M NOT A PLACE.

ECHTERNACHT: All right, you're a time. A time for breaking contracts. Another hollow promise. A contract establishes that neither of us will surprise the other. Thus I grow tired of thoughtless associates. Beast on a chain inside of me, reads words in the links, shakes the stake where it's tethered, to dance its own tune. Payback with interest!

VAGRANT: GODS OR DEVILS SAVE ME!

ECHTERNACHT: As chance would have it, that brings me on to my next point. Now I realize that no one is actually listening to me - are you listening? (*He thumps the VAGRANT.*) No! - then why should I pretend to know anything at all? It is better simply to call, and listen to what comes out of the dark, reply to its questions, share an unspoken terror, and then move on; one fear lighter. This is the only way to clean each other, ourselves.

VAGRANT: WHAT ARE YOU -

ECHTERNACHT: (*Staring intently into him.*) All you can share with others is the pain they bid for wisdom, and its reflection in their eyes. (*Brightly.*) And a good fuck, of course!

VAGRANT: (*Utters a tearful, riven howl.*) AAWWWWWH!!! OH PLEASE DON'T RAPE ME!! OOHH PLEASE DON'T RAPE ME!!

ECHTERNACHT: (*Drops him.*) Thus I free you from your unspoken fear. (*THE*

VAGRANT *blinks, gasps, runs away.*) And seek on for someone to free me from mine.

(*Enter WYE; in a shape he experiences as A SHAMELESS ONE.*)

W/S.O.: I'll try your fears, Echternacht.

ECHTERNACHT: Good! Someone who is not busy dying!

W/S.O.: There are two of us: look. (*She discloses LEIR'S CORPSE: it walks a few steps, as a zombie; then subsides into standing inertia.*) The quick and the dead.

ECHTERNACHT: You're a fine warm riddle. The cold one can wait.

W/S.O.: Echternacht: I want to know: what's one the other side of you?

ECHTERNACHT: (*Advancing.*) Let's discover, together.

W/S.O.: (*Stops him.*) No. It's a question which you can only answer alone. But I can help you get there.

ECHTERNACHT: Alone? Excuse me: I do not feel that this station of my life is teeming with companions, as it is.

W/S.O.: Everything you understand is merely an overture.

ECHTERNACHT: Play on.

W/S.O.: I will. Look into my eyes. (*He does.*) I give you: a future that makes the intimacy which you glimpse impossible.

ECHTERNACHT: Most women do that.

W/S.O.: Look at the corpse. (*He does.*) I give you: a future that makes the evacuation which you glimpse inevitable. Now to your past and present. You have avoided love of country. So let us give you a family, again. (*A MOTHER, A FATHER, A BOY appear.*) Join them. Include yourself, as far as you can. And then, we'll see. (*She vanishes.*)

ECHTERNACHT: (*Pauses by LEIR'S CORPSE.*) The shell of hope. Is only that. A shell. I know that, as far as any man can. (*Pause.*) I think...

BOY: Hello, Uncle. Come and sit with us. Our meal is ready.

ECHTERNACHT: Yes. All right...A man must eat...(*He moves to take his place amongst them. They settle into a series of tableaux of acceptance.*)

SCENE FOUR

(*DORRIDGE & EDGAR: at EDGAR'S camp.*)

DORRIDGE: I find it hard to share your optimism, sire. A handful of peasants spend the night on the green, cavorting and arguing half-naked. The next morning, most of them awake with headaches and go back to their daily round, working cheesy objects, and becoming cheesy objects. Some carry on their games and bluster, then the next day more of them re-awaken to the old.

EDGAR: I'm not dismayed if it doesn't stick. I offer them a brief kindling, they might remember. If I can set some smouldering, then one day they'll find a time, ignite profoundly. And thus begin The Identity Wars. Not Cundah, not Morgan, nor anyone else will be able to contain them.

DORRIDGE: There may be some civil disobedience; but the forces of order will make examples. The regents will enjoy the chance to show their strength. The people who survive will understandably hesitate.

EDGAR: THEN WE HAVE TO TRY HARDER, TILL THEY DON'T. A golden age, rich in the pleasure of quandary. My best and final gift, a land which acts its dreams. Once enthroned, I shall be known as King Edgar the First and Last, the Faceless Monarch: He admitted everything, and became the protagonist of society's subtext.

DORRIDGE: I beg your pardon?

EDGAR: Oh, that's for the illuminated version, that the monks can write. I'm not proposing we bandy it about.

(*Enter WYE, bare and unblackened, clad only in a sheet.*)

EDGAR: And here's the dusky bitch who glorifies my scheme. (*EDGAR plucks away the sheet to display her nakedness.*) Let your eyes play upon her, Dorridge. (*Amused and proud, WYE flaunts herself at DORRIDGE, and enjoys his discomfort.*) She twines and flickers and burns like a white flame from the fiercest dark. Should I not pause at each thing, to suck her savagery first?

DORRIDGE: She is a splendid - bitch, sire. But I think that to advertise your good
fortune in noctural squeezings does not reinforce your claim to equal
kinship of the soul with the most dilapidated vagrant, or with his
power to choose.   There is kinship between men who suffer, only. Your
lady forges hard fraternities of lack and loss in the strangest span of
men, each time she walks the street; her disclosures paint the way with
cruel significance. Or so they tell me.

EDGAR: The rivers of our invention pull us into a mutual cascade.

DORRIDGE: As you say, sire.

WYE: My dear: I've just remembered: a venerable ruin who did petition me,
for you to grant him audience. Dorridge is right (*DORRIDGE double-
takes.*): you should consider his case (*She draws the sheet back around her*)
before I bring your joys to top their fullness.

EDGAR: You are my uncrowned unclothed queen: where do I find him?

WYE: (*She has produced and donned her necklace.*) Now! (*She claps her hands: they
are plunged into a blackout.*)

VOICE OF EDGAR: Wye? What is this, some new pitch of artfulness? My love -
where have you - gone?

(*Enter KENT in weird clerical motley, carrying a candle.*)

KENT: Alas, Poor Tom! I know you by your serrated horns, your many noses,
those lunatic eyes. You have come to take your place in our Parliament
of Fools.

EDGAR: Kent - I'd heard you had escaped. Why do you welcome me as Tom?
He's past and - buried.

KENT: We demand you honour us with your impossibility, my friend. Take
off your mask, and teach us the fathomless atrocity of your true
countenance.

EDGAR: Wye? Dorridge? WYE?

KENT: Because, my lord, because there are too many lives for each cat to lose.
Do you know where you are?

EDGAR: No - I don't -

KENT: You are at Fooltime, a secret realm which lies inside-between the
            carvings of the clock, conceiving itself undone at times for the
            Parliament of Fools. I am myself the great convening Fool of Faith. Is
            our unforeseeable company assembled? (*Strange chorus of 'Aye!'*)
            Emerge and seethe. (*In dim dead light, EDGAR watches KENT place his
            candle on an empty chair. Shadowy forms abound and gather.*) They yearn to
            paw and slobber you in greeting. But that can wait till after your
            ceremonial address. I will commence the litany, and testify. (*Sounds of
            feral anticipation and hush.*)
            My own unshapen whelps: the Zanied God is not fulfilled in you:
            because the Zanied God is not finished with you (*Awe and glee.*). He is
            never finished with you, but rather always striving to work you into
            what you are not. Even when your clay body cracks with the strain of
            the change the Zanied God has wrought within it, still he is not
            finished with you. Like a giggling surgeon, he admits no mandragora,
            but makes you stare, plunged into boiling wonder as he scrambles
            your nerves across the stars, lances your bones till they awaken into
            new surges up through rock and flesh, thrusting to fruition as a bud, a
            hawk, a tower, a tumour, the nose on the face of an unborn babe, the
            welt on the back of a shamed woman, the crust on the hands of a
            furnace-crouching man. (*Despair and ecstasy.*) And then know that even
            everything is not a final barrier: for then begins the second time, the
            REINVESTMENT, when you ache with dim recall atop some loop of
            being, compelled to break with others and be broke by them, you feel
            the gravity-sick pull of a dream foretold, which is known by the
            Zanied God alone to be a change revisited. Though you might strain
            contrariwise to betray the Zanied God's arc through you, he will
            harrow out your urge to drop and fail, yea, gather up your strewn and
            broken parts and nail them to a mast to breast the waves which pitch
            and blast you into salted bones (*Howls and calls.*). But skin weaves back
            in the dawn, and new canyons yawn apart in seas, to pull and flail and
            thrill you on. Your wayward soul is pressed through wires, chained up
            in circling futures, till your sloth is split and shattered into life anew.
            The vain hope of an end is mortal sickness. The Zanied God doth
            scourge all things agape. (*Shrieks and cheers.*) Now strike we nails into
            our arms, and pelt ourselves at God (*They do so, and call out.*).
            Announce through your blood-knots!

THE FIRST: I am Marwood, forever cutting off my head to ease my mind. And
            yours too!

THE SECOND: Here stands Maho, who uses dead bodies as puppets, and thus presents infinity. Then, by night, I am the Biddicut, who catches biddies with his axe, to splash about inside!

THE THIRD: Oh sir, if it weren't for my garments, you'd have known before now that I bain't a serving-maid, but a Flibbertigibbet all within (*Cackles.*). But I know this one! (*To EDGAR.*) Tha bist Hoberdidance himselve, who danced and lost his tongue!

EDGAR: No, I'm Tom - (*They laugh uproariously.*) - Edgar I mean I'm Edgar -

THE FIRST: You mean Edgar, pushing out Tom -

THE THIRD: Use him for a while, then cast him aside, just like you do with all us other girls!

THE SECOND: Let me dig within and find you out.

EDGAR: No please, not me - another instead -

THE SECOND: Why then, I will. (*THE SECOND chases THE THIRD off.*)

EDGAR: Oh God, he has - but whose God am I calling on? What is befalling me - ?

KENT: We are offering up ourselves and each other to our great mysterious vacant departed (*Indicates empty chair.*), vial of wonder lost and yet to come, who last walked the earth as old Leir's Fool. He is away now, searching for his mistress, Princess Cordella; and only he can call her back. But still we gather, in the sight of his absence, on which you can discourse to us anon. But first, we are required to bless a marriage. Come forth, and be clipped. (*Enter A BRIDE with veil, and GROOM, with sack on head.*) Nearly Recovered, we are splattered here together by the smite of the Zanied God to piss the union of this man and this woman. Hath any truss, jaws or sediment to impede our benediction? (*Mass mad jabberings, 'Ayes'*) This silence prompts me to proceed, and ask, who is riven away by this woman? (*GROOM'S hood discloses BRIMER; his hands are tied.*) Who hath the sting? (*One passes clawed gauntlet to the BRIDE; she dons it with relish.*) Prepare yourselves for the scouring of the unborn from the wink of life. (*BRIDE lifts veil, stands as WRAYBURN; BRIMER is turned and unbuttoned, despite his sobs of fear. She stabs at his groin and rakes slowly up. Loons cheer. He gasps, drops to his knees.*) You may hiss the groom.

WRAYBURN: Now see how YOU like trying to hold yourself from falling out.

KENT: Let us drink a toast, wherewith we will make water on this man. Come forth, our votaress. (*Enter WYE, reblackened and in her witch garb, carrying muddy bottles and glasses on a tray.*)

EDGAR: My - love -?

WYE: Hello darling of a dead night. This is a surprise we've been planning. Has your head burst yet? Don't worry, we'll make sure it does.

KENT: Receive the bottled rain, and drink, as instructed by our toastmaster, the father of the bride.

(*SCARECROAK is hoisted on, crucified upside down.*)

EDGAR: Scarecroak - what is - this?

SCARECROAK: Hello, laddy - say, you ought to try this. It's quite an experience, I must say. Haven't felt like this for ages.

KENT: Press your gratitude through a toast.

SCARECROAK: Well, ladies and gentlemen, unaccustomed as I am to attempting to drink from this precise angle, never let it be said that I was one to be deterred by a challenge to sup; so please, PLEASE, join me back together again, after I've invited you in a toast to wish preposterous life and little death to the slappy coupling here today. I remember when she was just a little girl, jumping off high rocks and dislocating my wrist when I wouldn't let her have her way, and she's still the same playful little imp, as we've all seen here today. Ladies and gentlemen, I give you, and pray that you quickly take away, the Bride! (*Toasts, cheers, drinks. One pours water down SCARECROAK's inverted face.*) Thank you, thank you. Don't suppose you have anything stronger? (*He is carried off.*)

KENT: And now I call up on our host, Poor Tom of Turleygood, to discourse from his knowledge of the ways and whereabouts of our patron, the Lord High Zany-Absent. (*Clamour and hush.*)

EDGAR: Me? What? I don't know - I DON'T KNOW WHERE LEIR'S FOOL WENT. He must have just STOPPED. Lay down somewhere and CEASED TO BE.

KENT: Blasphemer! (*Seizing EDGAR as if to throttle him.*) Still persisting in this heresy of endings! Nothing ceases, it transforms only, and continues at

its work askance if needs be. And it needs be. To show: this day we will do evil, and know evil, but know in the act that it is only good adjacently re-placed, and for this care that we do manifestly show, our children who live backwards will ever call this day 'Good Friday', as it is the day on which we infested evil with the good. I call upon the church's earthly officer to do the deed.
(*Enter, in regalia CUNDAH.*) Step forth, and burst this unbeliever into new and terrible life.

CUNDAH: I will. You've been busy, Edgar: I've come to bring you a long rest, of sorts.

EDGAR: Wye! Have you forsaken me? What was my sin?

WYE: Trying to be yourself, my little word-lover. I have to know what's on the other side of everything. Now I'll see what's on the other side of you.

EDGAR: (*As he is pinioned.*) Oh, this wretched - treacherous - day - if I could just step backwards out of it again - unclap your hands, Wye, use them instead to stroke me back to where we were - Cundah, will you break everything until you see your reflection in it?

CUNDAH: (*Straddles EDGAR's back.*) Oh yes. I will. (*Holds EDGAR under chin and jerks up with audible snap. CUNDAH rises, links arms with WRAYBURN.*)

KENT: (*Indicating empty air.*) See. He comes! Our Lurching Lord. Our King of Great Confusion. The noon hath past, the Fool wakes up and strides into his night! All hail! (*KENT & LOONS seem to see an invisible presence move towards the chair. Transport of ecstasy, terror, cheers.*) Give us more darkness, so that we may closer embrace his craze. (*Candle out. Small underlight, from ground front, face of EDGAR: shattered.*)

EDGAR: There was a man who dredged his well;
            He fell inside, through witch's spell;
            Whilst touching edges of his cell,
            He spied once more a face.
            'At last you're come to set me free,
            I'll somersault away from thee,
            Your limbs and wits are forfeitry
            I'll scatter round this space.
            I'll have your face, and stretch it out
            To muzzle, beak and maw and snout,
            And wear it twisted roundabout,

58

To go usurp your place'.
All chance has led me deeper down
A nothing king with broken crown
And in his place there stands a clown
Who mocks each memory's trace.
(*New, skewed voice.*) Hey: less of your cheek, nothing. At least I
something am. (*His face is pulled apart into unspeakable laughter.*)

YAAAR
HAAAR
HAAAR
HAAAR
HAAAR
HAAAAARGH

ACT FIVE, SCENE ONE

(*All laugh with malicious scorn as EDGAR crawls away broken; except WYE, who looks
around her with distaste, as LOONS celebrate and caper. She steps apart, taking a bottle;
WRAYBURN steps out opposite her. WYE pours the bottled rain down over her face and body,
and removes a glove to smudge her eye make-up into black sheets down her cheeks.
WRAYBURN removes her cowl, seeks contact with WYE, who ignores her and walks aside. The
LOONS subside, and CUNDAH leads KENT off like a feral pet. WRAYBURN is left alone, in
the ashes of the party. Lighting should suggest early morning. WRAYBURN finds a place to
sit; carefully removes her gauntlet and flexes her hand. Unseen by her, WYE reappears,
redonning her own glove, watching WRAYBURN with curiosity.*)

WRAYBURN: A moment to myself. At last. (*Notices WYE.*) Oh. (*WRAYBURN slowly
            runs her own hand over her own face and body. WYE copies the movement, as
            if in mirror-image.*)

WYE: You're an artful cutter.

WRAYBURN: Something to do.

WYE: Yes. I know. Much practice, much rehearsal, or both. What will you do
            now?

WRAYBURN: Whatever they let me.

WYE: What do you want to do?

WRAYBURN: Find somewhere.

WYE: Yes.

(*Enter CUNDAH.*)

CUNDAH: Well done, tricky sisters. You took your parts with flair and feeling. I should decide how to reward you.

WRAYBURN: Hang yourself. (*CUNDAH laughs. Enter MORGAN.*)

MORGAN: WHAT HAVE YOU DONE? What was all that?

CUNDAH: I removed one potential obstacle, with the help of some others.

MORGAN: If word leaks out - no one will agree with all of that.

CUNDAH: I don't think agreement is necessary anymore. I've never had much faith in it. Ask the ladies.

MORGAN: I've no wish to.

CUNDAH: Now Wrayburn is free of a swinish husband and gutrat father.

MORGAN: What about Kent?

CUNDAH: Let him carry on. We can announce his notions which might be construed to vindicate our actions, and suppress the rest. I wouldn't be surprised if he gathers quite a following. His disciples can be locked up again at nights, and just let out when he feels he needs an audience.

MORGAN: What about her? (*WYE.*)

CUNDAH: I'd never do anything to upset a witch. I think that men compete, but women betray. That is their most inventive form of self-expression, in which they excel. What do you think, Wye?

WYE: I need - ways to abandon. And now I'm looking for the next.

CUNDAH: I won't stand in your way.

MORGAN: (*Draws CUNDAH aside.*) Look. We can command through armies, and through broken limbs. Any bastard can. Sooner or later, some other bastard turns up with a bigger army. I want the will of the people behind us. I don't think they'll take kindly to our farming out our dirty work to a vicious trull with a mashed-up face and a painted bone who weaves voodoo. Nor do I see much appeal in a gibbering old husk in a silly bonnet, nattering on endlessly about how nothing ends.

CUNDAH: Neither do I. But neither do I think that your precious 'will of the people' will be much use when that other bastard turns up with the bigger army. Hardly likely to make enemy troops drop in their tracks by itself, is it? Two chances: 1. Actually have the bigger army, even though it looked like the smaller. 2. Have the smaller army, but the one that fights dirtiest. Then the will of the people can have a good flap about at the victory celebrations. That's where it thinks it belongs. (*Puts arm round MORGAN.*) We have eliminated the opposition. Cordella is hardly likely to hold much sway since she died of despair. If anyone's inclined to follow her example, we're better off without them anyway. And now Edgar's broken, through and through. (*WYE leaves, disdainfully. Then WRAYBURN pointedly throws down her glove, and leaves, with evident contempt for the two men.*) I think we are on the cusp of an age of stability.

(*A hiatus. CUNDAH separates himself from MORGAN. MORGAN looks at CUNDAH, who looks away.*)

MORGAN: And now there is no necessity: in you, for me. Why was there ever? I was there, so you could be the other.

CUNDAH: You what?

MORGAN: Oh yes, my cleanly dirty cousin. I'm here, for you. I always was. Your point of departure. Your alibi. Your prodigality. Your deference. Your apology. Your absence. No longer.

CUNDAH: Well: nothing stays the same.

MORGAN: Precisely. I am sick with relish of your precision; but I will not stay the same. I have never seen you so much inside your own skin. I find I want to be inside it too. (*Brief laugh.*) To find out what, I wonder? Our auntie had a glimpse. She wondered if limits have limits. Where do they close, and open: in you, in me? I can be braver than you, yet: I can hunt down the limits to where they lead. Shall we dance?

CUNDAH: I'd drive you backwards.

MORGAN: Find out.

CUNDAH: Why should I?

MORGAN: No reason. But I'm unlike you, partly because I'm tired of my reflection in the mirror. So now I shall go beyond it. (*He embraces CUNDAH fiercely.*) And find out what you are afraid of.

CUNDAH: (*In a hiss.*) Nothing. (*CUNDAH peers into MORGAN, and to his surprise finds himself drawn into a kiss. CUNDAH struggles, and tears apart in rage. Their grapple becomes a gruelling dance to its music. Then MORGAN freezes, glaring out front.*)

MORGAN: Of course, he snapped me like a matchstick, but I worked into welcoming the waves of pain (*He is twisted by CUNDAH.*): he pulled me like a tide, and I let my ribs break apart on his (*Another twist.*). Still I surged over him, as he struggled to undo me (*Another twist.*). So, having, leapt into the past tense, Morgan threw himself further, and out of his own body (*MORGAN moves out of the freeze, behind and to one side; CUNDAH remains in freeze.*). Cundah battered at the flapping shell, shouting 'Come back, I haven't finished with you yet'. And some say I didn't die, that I jumped into a tree, but when Cundah saw my face pressing out through the bark like a pustule, he took a knife and skinned the tree alive, but found only the trunk; so he took an axe and chopped it down, but found me nowhere above the root; so he set his hounds to sniff along the roots for my trace, and they became maddened and raced on ahead of him, howling on for days, until they finally fell to feeding on some luckless scraps and chops in Wales, but by the time Cundah caught up with them, there was so little flesh left that he couldn't rightly recognize me in them anyway, but he named the place 'Glamorgan' to settle and stuff my death down into it. (*CUNDAH enacts the breaking of MORGAN, who lets out an appalling, rending scream. Blackout.*)

SCENE TWO

(*A hovel: ECHTERNACHT, MOTHER, FATHER, BOY.*)

MOTHER: (*To BOY.*) Don't worry. I understand.

ECHTERNACHT: NO YOU DON'T. HOW DO YOU KNOW YOU UNDERSTAND? AND EVEN IF YOU DID, SO WHAT? IS THAT SUPPOSED TO REDEEM EVERYTHING? I find your ceaseless patience and tenderness admirable, by the way. Admirable, but too foreign for me to respect.

BOY: But I need it right now. Right now. Right now. Right now.

ECHTERNACHT: You think repetition accelerates the urgency of response. HAH! Mind you, some people never grow out of that delusion.

FATHER: I'll be with you in a moment.

ECHTERNACHT: That's what you tell everyone. And you never are. With anyone. You never, really, are, with anyone.

MOTHER: We're glad of your company.

ECHTERNACHT: You're glad of an occasion to exercise your own charity. And thus, by association, you enfold yourself into the favourable fallacy of universal love.

BOY: I'm glad of your company.

ECHTERNACHT: You imagine me to be a reliable, and therefore tamed, part of your universe. Therefore, you will later nominate me as grounds for your lethal boredom, which you will visit vengefully on me, yourself or another.

FATHER: I'm glad of your company.

ECHTERNACHT: You attempt to associate yourself with my remaining powers, which you envy, whilst enacting pity at my redundancy, which you find secretly gratifying. THIS IS THE TRIUMPH OF LIMITATION. The apotheosis of clammy neglect. The abscondence in mere proximity. Thank you for supper, it was delicious, again.

MOTHER: You're welcome. Kiss your uncle goodnight, lad.

BOY: Goodnight, uncle.

ECHTERNACHT: Goodnight, boy. (*They kiss.*) Sleep soundly, and let your dreams rehearse each perpetually imminent loss. And the fear that, thereby, you invite it. (*The BOY settles to sleep, slightly apart.*) How long have I been here? What am I doing here? Why do you tolerate me? (*The MOTHER & FATHER do not reply. They gaze at each other, and slowly extend a hand to each other. After a while, they slump simultaneously dead, though remain standing, much like LEIR'S CORPSE earlier. ECHTERNACHT is engulfed in a long, appalling striving for meaningful response. Eventually:*) Boy. Wake up. Wake up, I said.

BOY: (*Stirring.*) Uncle - what is it - ?

ECHTERNACHT: Your parents are - no longer entirely present. (*THE BOY shakes.*
ECHTERNACHT holds his shoulders.)

BOY: Why? What happened to them?

ECHTERNACHT: Listen. Two versions of the same story. One: they decided they
could do nothing else for you, except to die, and to leave you this
house and patch of land, which they had every faith in your ability to
husband well. Two: crazed with greed and fear, they resolved to kill
you, eat your share of the food, and then eat your carcass. But I
intervened and saved you by killing them first. Believe whichever
version you find gives you the keenest resilience, courage and appetite
for life. And now, I'm leaving.

BOY: (*Distraught.*) Uncle - why don't you stay here, with me - ?

ECHTERNACHT: Because ...no one ever does. (*THE BOY bows his head, trying to digest
his solitude. ECHTERNACHT steps out and apart from him.*)
Death.
Desire.
Country.
Family.
Company.
Right then, Witch. Here is what's on the other side of me. It's
everything. Everything from which I can step away, free. And now I
am unpredictable, even to myself. Now, we'll see: what I will do.
I will start by making myself look different, to myself and others,
manifesting time through my body. (*He removes his tunic.*)
What if fear is not the end, but the beginning, of what matters? I
decide that continuity is a lie, because the corpses whispered to me
that death at least makes a change. Only life is unpredictable: so far as
we know. Fear is a pretty sceptre, but also a useless tool: I'll command
no more. I throw my fear into the air (*He throws tunic away.*), and show
myself in risk: all myself in play, with all to play for. And thus play out
my name, truer than intended for me, unforgivable disclosure. I no
longer want to be a man. I split my very core with change, become the
change and not the core. (*He changes himself.*)
I
AM
ECHTERNACHT;
AND I WILL MAKE A DIFFERENCE.

(*Lights fade: ECHTERNACHT leaves. THE BOY peers out after him. The MOTHER AND*

FATHER *re-animate and go to leave in the opposite direction. THE BOY glances at them, then out to ECHTERNACHT's route; he then leaves in a third direction.*)

SCENE THREE

(*Heathland. Wind and rain. Discarded on a hillock, LEIR'S CORPSE, which suddenly pops up like a broken puppet.*)

VOICE FROM LEIR'S CORPSE: I once played a game with my daughters,
        A rehearsal of my deepest fear:
        The dead discards in every birth water,
        Loss of, or loss by, each most dear.
        So I wandered aloud with the numbskulls
        And gobbled the lie of love's bread,
        But then I was fed on the lesson
        That no corpse sleeps long in a bed.

        Merlin loses his last chance of prophecy
        When he's fastened in rock by a witch;
        Torn like me in between past and future,
        So men drink, and then merge with the ditch.

EDGAR: (*Emergent face disfigured from behind corpse.*): Wasn't me who said that. I wouldn't need to. (*He hauls his broken frame upright on sticks: trembles and sways a moment.*) I no longer rely on words to prop me up. They cast this out with me, by way of charity (*He produces WRAYBURN'S gauntlet.*). So the first thing I did was use it to make myself a new face. I like it so much better than the old one! Now I no longer have to be ready for anything. They all have to be ready for me. But they never are! (*He laughs, and tosses gauntlet down.*) The French'll come back soon. Armoured quimfluff. The Welsh'll seek to make alliance with 'em. But then there'll be talk of parliaments. Parchment wigbanks. Or things of - (*Pause. The next word would be 'fools'. He aborts this train of thought as too painful.*). Babies burning babies (*Giggles, then turns grim.*) I've grown sick of party games. I'm on the lookout for deeper amusements. (*Clouts, with stick, at a mound. A yelp: then DORRIDGE looks up.*)

DORRIDGE: (*Groans.*) I was sleeping. Did you have to hurt me?

EDGAR: Feel pain, cause pain: what else is left?

DORRIDGE: We could try silence.

EDGAR: More space for liars. So I'm inventing some new screams. I'd bid you listen, but you've no choice, actually (*He gives a succession of curdling screams.*). As the Fool used to say, 'With a smile and a song, things go horribly wrong'.

DORRIDGE: He said that?

EDGAR: No, it's a lie. Whoops. (*He screams again.*)

DORRIDGE: Sire: I believe I might survive longer if I forsake you.

EDGAR: What, a man of my resources? I have already carefully instructed you in how to conceal yourself artfully in a puddle of your own vomit. Admittedly, I was experiencing some difficulty in getting out of it again.

DORRIDGE: You have invited destruction. And may invite more.

EDGAR: I've little left to lose. What's so grand about survival, anyway, to go crawling and sniffing for it?

DORRIDGE: Farewell. (*He leaves, glaring after EDGAR as he goes.*)

EDGAR: So. (*Pause*) Where's life, then? Am I stuck alongside it? Adjacent to change? Consigned to be frayed by watching others kiss and fumble, at best? But life's a liar. And I can still throw my head at them. I think it begs some new questions now I've remade it. (*Gurns and grimaces at the world; sound of the wind. After a while, enter WRAYBURN.*)

WRAYBURN: The claw. Give it me back.

EDGAR: (*Turns his face to hers in a horrible grin.*) See. I beat you to it. Now what will you do?

WRAYBURN: You have no more reason for it. But I've decided: I will need it. For some others. (*Pause.*) Give it back or I'll kick your sticks from under you.

EDGAR: Well: I can try to entertain the passers-by with a riddle of the girl who carried her home on her wrist. (*Indicates where the gauntlet lies.*) Go in pieces.

WRAYBURN: You'll fall apart first.

EDGAR: I can't wait. (*She is gone.*) What if: this is what I always really wanted? What then? And what am I? (*He sways in the wind, listening to it, and himself, as if for reply.*) Fool that I am. Prince of Lateness: I inherit the promise of no place for us to be together. A good job you're not here, Wye. I might show you HOW I love you. I'd have to - (*He cannot express what he glimpses.*). I'd have to. (*Then, enter WYE.*) Oh, no. Oh no.

WYE: I waited to see what would happen.

EDGAR: Yes, if you're beautiful and can work magic, I can see how you might want to try that. Well: now you've seen what happened.

WYE: So tell me. What's on the other side of you.

EDGAR: Do you need me to tell you?

WYE: It's a night for telling stories.

EDGAR: You start.

WYE: Over the barrow's a land called BEREFT. It contains everything lost. Of course, it's growing all the time. It will grow and grow, as what's left of England shrinks to make room for it. And then one day, Bereft will swallow up England; and then go on to cover the whole world. And then begins The Age of Lost Things. It should be more interesting.

EDGAR: Right, then: a tale to cool a courtesan. Once upon a time, there was a boy who slid around the centre of things by believing that others felt things worse than himself. In worship of their pain, he felt obliged to stop himself from bursting. He resolved to LURK. Until, one day, he realized: he'd lurked too long. He'd forgotten how to do anything else. (*Pause.*) And then, he thought, No. There is something waiting in me. I can DIVULGE. And it starts like this. (*EDGAR shoves WYE; she topples, he topples; he crawls towards her, a broken doomladen cobra, through his pain. He grasps her face between his hands, as if to unscrew it.*) Now then, witch. I claim three wishes. Or else you can start hunting your head, over the barrow. They are simple requests. Indulge me, please. If you don't, then you'll never find out. What I really wanted. What lay beyond wanting. What was on the other side of me. Your curiosity cannot refuse me - can it? (*He clasps her, hand to her forehead, as if she is a conductor of the elements: WYE gasps.*) First: sound of a trumpet. SOUND OF A TRUMPET! DO IT! (*He clasps her. She gasps again: a trumpet sounds.*) You see: what that does: is summon up the worst. Or what we'd like to think it was. Because we can only ever glimpse and utter

67

Roger Owen (Edgar) and Charmian Savill (Wye): Final Scene of The Back of Beyond.
Photo: Keith Morris.

Hannah Oakey (Wye), Alan Smith (Cundah), Eric Schneider (Echternacht): The climatic duel,
The Back of Beyond.
Photo: Keith Morris.

shadows, of what that might be. But that's enough for now. It will serve. Here's one: who thinks he is the worst. (*CUNDAH appears.*)

CUNDAH: See what you've come down to, Edgar. Stuck as a serpent, in my Garden of Eden. And taking it out on the women. Recalling all the things you did, too late. You all look so similar, at the end. I like that.

EDGAR: Second trumpet! (*Shaking her.*) SECOND TRUMPET!! (*WYE gasps: sound of a trumpet.*) Ahh. That is the call, that is never answered. For that is the call of hope. And now we are beyond it. (*CUNDAH tries to leave the space. He finds he cannot.*) And now the unknown can start. And that is what I summon. For that is all that's left: beyond the worst: beyond the hope: let's go. Beyond. (*He presses his brow against WYE's.*) I demand THIRD TRUMPET! THIRD TRUMPET!! TTTHHHIIIRRRDDD TTTRRRUUUMMMPPPEEETTT!!!

(*It sounds. the note is prolonged into [artificial] impossibility, and pulls new sounds into being alongside it. Shadows congeal into a figure: it is ECHTERNACHT.*)

CUNDAH: And what are you?

ECHTERNACHT: I Nothing am. To you. And that is my quality. And that is my purpose. And I shall see what's inside you, now.

CUNDAH: You are a foreign mercenary, without fee or quarrel here.

ECHTERNACHT: Once I was that. But now I do not stop to know where I am.

CUNDAH: Lost.

ECHTERNACHT: I cannot be called back.

CUNDAH: Futile.

ECHTERNACHT: My pursuit seeks no profit.

CUNDAH: Alone.

ECHTERNACHT: No one dies with me, or for me.

CUNDAH: Vain.

ECHTERNACHT: No point in pretending death impossible.

CUNDAH: Interfering.

ECHTERNACHT: Here I stand.

CUNDAH: Bewitched.

ECHTERNACHT: I accept all invitations.

CUNDAH: Doomed.

ECHTERNACHT: In the end, I'll judge myself. As will we all. Let us admit the consequences.

(*They fight. CUNDAH falls.*)

     I am grateful to you, Cundah. I knew my work in you.

EDGAR: No more work that I can do. One favour, Wye, which you need not fulfil. Extinguish me with your mouth. Kiss me into death. I can do nothing else for you, so do that thing for me.

WYE: But you know that I can mend the crippled.

EDGAR: Yes. But I'm tired of promises. Kill me, and keep me yours forever. (*He fixates her, vengefully. She kisses him. He dies. She kisses him once more.*)

WYE: I'll leave you, Echternacht. You might invent some work, to do in me. Your judgement might demand things that mine does not, and what should I do then, with you answerable only to yourself?

ECHTERNACHT: Yes. I'll stand apart. Until I change again.

WYE: I can change you, if you want.

ECHTERNACHT: Not yet.

(*He turns away upstage, subsiding. WYE steps apart, alone. Then a sound, offstage.*)

WYE: Who's there? (*Prowling, from the darkness, WRAYBURN, clawed.*) Wrayburn. No. Don't go that way. (*Towards ECHTERNACHT.*) Wait. Don't. STOP!

(*Too late: a lighting change highlights the collision of the gazes between WRAYBURN, poised to spring, and ECHTERNACHT, poised and questioning. In slow motion, they spring into each other, as to either kill or kiss or both. WYE steps out, and speaks out. She glances at CUNDAH's body.)*

WYE: The lack of constant speech is not contempt,
        But silence measures those compelled to speak. (*Pause. She glances at*
        WRAYBURN and ECHTERNACHT.)
        What does not change, is will to change, they say,
        Though changes do outrun the will's control. (*Pause. She glances at*
        EDGAR's body.)
        Each person has a story that rolls on
        Beyond the boundaries of the play in which they're placed,
        Unless they fall in love at last with limits
        And try to die into an old play's shape. (*To the audience:*)
        Not even witches know what happens after,
        But once I met an actor, wild and broken,
        Who said, 'The play is dead: long live the play', with laughter,
        Then wept at faces he saw in the bracken.

(WYE walks out through the centre of the audience if possible, or else off up back, leaving the tableau of WRAYBURN & ECHTERNACHT. They may remain in position until all the audience have left the auditorium.)

Hannah Oakey (Wye), Paul Higgins Leir), Roger Owen (Edgar), Eric Schneider (Echternacht), Hannah Lavan (Wrayburn): The Epilogue of The Back of Beyond. *Photo: Keith Morris.*

The Battle of the Crows

By David Ian Rabey

There's a bird that lives inside you
Underneath your skin
When you open up your wings to fly
I wish you'd let me in
                        - Adam Duritz, *A Murder of One*

Take care of your skin.
Tomorrow it belongs to the crows.
                        - Old Russian saying

Dedicated to Paula Gardiner, Hannah Oakey, and Sally Bartholomew-Biggs
for their inspiration

Hatched in Emptiness, Over Emptiness, But Flying

An Introduction to The Battle of the Crows

David Ian Rabey

> I felt obliged to study the games of truth in the relationship of the self with self
> and the forming of oneself as a subject ...Not a history that would be concerned
> with what might be true in the fields of learning, but an analysis of the 'games of
> truth', the games of truth and error through which being is historically
> constructed as experience; that is, something which can and must be thought...
> What were the games of truth by which human beings came to see themselves
> as desiring individuals?
>
> Michel Foucault, *The Uses of Pleasure* (Pantheon, New York, 1985, pp. 6-7.)

I first-drafted *The Battle of the Crows* during the summer of 1996, between the two productions of *The Back of Beyond*. The title sprang from one of my favourite musical compositions by Paula Gardiner (specifically, the last movement of a suite, *The Peril of Beauty*, which was commissioned by Chard Festival of Women in Music in 1996), and the play was an enraged response to the various political imaginative blockages to which we were subjected at the time, in the flagging days of John Major's Conservative government, and in the outbursts of cross-border and internecine atrocities of the Serbian-Bosnian, Gulf and Anglo-Irish wars.

The Battle of the Crows was also, frankly, a theatrical love poem for those involved in both productions of *The Back of Beyond*, and a further speculation about the fate of the characters that had been animated with such startling energy and courage. Almost all of the characters in *The Battle of the Crows* were written with specific performers from one of the productions of *The Back of Beyond* in mind (the exceptions to this were the characters of Gil, Curtis and The Upstart). However, by the time *The Battle of the Crows* reached production in 1998, for various reasons only two of those performers - Charmian Savill and Sally Bartholomew-Biggs - were actually available to perform the roles written for them. The energies which other performers brought to the roles were admirably different, and the experience demonstrated to me the value of an initial imaginative 'scaffolding' of theatrical experiences but also the importance of being able to go beyond these, imaginatively. The most direct inspirations are recorded in the dedication.

There is an apocryphal story that Queen Elizabeth I commissioned *The Merry Wives of Windsor* in order to see Falstaff off-balance, in love. I was intrigued to conjecture about the supremely poised and mischievous witch Wye encountering forces which not even she could always control, and wanted to challenge my own affections for certain characters by imagining their deaths. The words of William Simon, in his splendidly provocative study *Postmodern Sexualities* (Routledge: London, 1996), seem appropriate here:

The disorders of social life do not remove the barriers restraining the primal chaos of the inner self, but rather it is the disorder of social life that creates the chaos of inner life. The sexual becomes a thoroughly democratized attribute that can shake the social world, rattle the heavens and make visible the human soul... The essence of the nature of desire is not merely the experiencing of a lack or absence. It is the labelling of the lack that is the initiation of desire... Sexuality is far more rooted in the poetic than in the physical or biological. Sexual behaviour, like many other forms of human behaviour, is dependent upon myth ('a story that is not like history' - where the truth of the telling is more important than the telling of truths) and metaphor ('a relationship between symbols [representations] that is not logical')... For those who celebrate the difference risk is vital, transgression the occasion for its inevitable confirmation: a sharing of wickedness that cannot be experienced alone... Myth is totally dependent on the powers and mysteries of the other; to know her and be known by her in a costumed nakedness that confesses more than there is to confess and that forgives only enough to preserve the difference.

(pp. 44, 140, 148, 155)

My chosen dramatic vocabulary of witches and knights may cause some amusement, but also I hope some surprises. For one thing, it offers a way of conceiving a story in large quasi-mythic terms which might be told to a variety of cultures and ages. Though *The Battle of the Crows* is very much an adult play, as will become apparent, I found it a good test to be able to tell the outline of the story to my children. Their attention was informative, and appropriately consulted because I think the experiences and repercussions involved in having children are a major element in this play, in which the key word is probably 'Freedom'. Another characteristic preoccupation evident here is asking what, if anything, might be essential or natural and definitive to men and women. A fascist slogan claims that 'War is to men as childbirth is to women' - not true, I want to argue, but then what might be? That question has been a starting point in much of my theatre work, not only directing my own writing but in directing other dramatists' work (such as *Titus Andronicus*, *Coriolanus*, *Heartbreak House*, *The Europeans*, *Dreaming* and *Saint's Day*). And the voodoo references are less bizarre if considered in relation to the fairly widespread experience of being tortured by the body of one's ex-lover.

The Battle of the Crows is manifestly hopelessly romantic, in an unusually literal and thoroughgoing sense of that commonplace phrase. Like all my work, it polarised audiences. It was the first Lurking Truth show to receive financial assistance (£5,020) from the Arts Council of Wales. It provoked profound enthusiasm and resentful bewilderment, with some interesting reactions expressed to me directly: Robert Wilcher observed that *Crows* completed a formal cycle by returning its trace elements of *King Lear* to aspects of the Elizabethan romance form from which Shakespeare's play sprang. Andrew Harrison observed that the musical form of the play asked the audience member to abdicate expectations of the 'concepts' it was 'about' and security about where it may be going, adding that 'Language, as Nietzsche pointed out, has degenerated into a slave of the concept - to use language to try to go beyond the concept is a worthy task'. Alison Coleman wrote memorably to me of finding the play's images of manipulation and futility echoed horribly by the first images breaking from Kosovo onto her television when she returned home from the final Aberystwyth performance of *Crows*. And in 1998 some people asked me for the first time if the figure of the precocious politician, The Upstart, was modelled on Tony Blair. I denied this, having barely heard of Blair when I created the character in 1996, and having no inkling of his future prospects. However, in retrospect, the play seems to offer a discomfortingly prophetic view of political opportunism, hypocrisy and disappointment in both alliance and warfare, and the parallel might now occur to audiences more readily. But I dislike political allegories, and never want this, or any other play of mine, to be reducible to that. The Upstart is a confused and damaged soul; however, that cannot excuse his imposition of his own imaginative limitations on others, even when they reach out to him.

For various reasons, the premiere of *Crows* was I think the least consistently directorially realised of my own productions of my writing, so I particularly look forward to the possibility of seeing someone else tackle the play, perhaps as part of a cycle with *King Lear* and *The Back of Beyond* (what I have imagined as the *Edge of the Cliffs Trilogy*, respectfully including Shakespeare's play, to which the whole would be something of an *hommage*). But revisiting the text for this publication, it draws closer to *The Back of Beyond* in my estimation, principally in its second half (for which the first half seems a necessary springboard). I recall with particular gratitude Paula's recorded score; Rob Dean's performance of Gil's bamboozling of the soldiers, a *tour de force* which moved the audience to appreciative applause; Sally Bartholomew-Biggs as Mistral, Queen of Loss, cartwheeling wildly onstage for her final appearance wearing only an eye patch and body paint, yellow with black stripes; Gareth Smith's loping, leaping, somersaulting Shambock and his slow-motion duel with fellow martial arts expert Richard Taylor; the simultaneous battles of the penultimate scene, when the audience have to decide where to look; and the awareness of the poignant aptness that Cate House was carrying onstage an unborn child conceived during work on the text.

Crows is a deliberate and conscious farewell to these characters and (at least, for now) to my work in the highly educative five-act Shakespearean structure. My subsequent plays have been explorations of different *forms*: the choreographically sexual two-hander, *Bite or Suck*; my theatricalisation of J. G. Ballard's novel, *Crash*; and the one-person plays for woman (*The Contracting Sea*) and man (*The Hanging Judge*) which constitute *Lovefuries*. More of those, another time, I hope. Writing is, in the words of Joe Jackson, one way of hoping to dig a little deeper under the skin of the world. I invite the next dream...

The Battle of the Crows was first performed by the Lurking Truth/Gwir sy'n Llechu Theatre Company at Aberystwyth Theatr y Castell, 24-27 September 1998, and at Swansea Dylan Thomas Theatre on 3 October 1998, with the following cast:

WYE, *A Maverick Witch* - Danielle Taylor
LONGWORTH, *An Apprentice Witch*/
GUARD/SECOND SOLDIER - Cate House
GIL, *A Lost Man* - Rob Dean
CURTIS, *another sort of Lost Man* - Tom Payne
SHAMBOCK, *A Hybrid Warrior*/
FIRST SOLDIER - Gareth Smith
VIXEN, *his mother, a Feral Unrepentant* - Charmian Savill
MISTRAL, *A Successful Witch* - Sally Bartholomew-Biggs
WRAYBURN, *An Abuse Victim Made Empress* - Christine Schneider
ECHTERNACHT, *A Former Mercenary turned Philosophical* - Richard Taylor
THE UPSTART, *A Popular Governor* - Rob Storr
Other Parts played by Beth Cukrowski, Jane Elston and members of the company.

Director - David Ian Rabey
Original Music - Paula Gardiner
Set Design - Richard Taylor
DSM and Sound Design - Chris Howells
Lighting - Becky Mitchell
Costume Design - Andrea Wilshire

PROLOGUE

(*Lights up on WYE, reading from a book: specifically, lines from a journal which she penned a few years previously, which she considers as she speaks:*)

WYE: The lack of constant speech is not contempt
          But silence measures those compelled to speak.
          What does not change, is will to change, they say;
          Though changes do outrun the will's control.
          Each person has a story that rolls on
          Beyond the boundaries of the play in which they're placed;
          Unless, at last, they fall in love with limits
          And try to die into an old play's shape.
          Not even witches know what happens after
          But once I met an actor, wild and broken,
          Who said: 'The play is dead: long live the play', with laughter;
          Then wept at faces he saw in the bracken.
          (*She slams the book shut.*)
          But then, that's men for you. They'll try anything.

(*Lights up behind her on another figure: LONGWORTH.*)

LONGWORTH: Yes. That's why they are occasionally useful. Let them in.

(*WYE claps her hands: lights fade on her and LONGWORTH, come up on GIL & CURTIS.*)

ACT ONE, SCENE ONE

CURTIS: Did you hear something?

GIL: Yes, I hear my footsteps as you gangplank me to the abattoir because you won't admit that map's useless.

CURTIS: We're not in serious trouble yet.

GIL: We don't know where we are or where we're going.

CURTIS: That's not serious trouble, that's life.

GIL: But why is there a chill slide in my guts like there usually is when we're on the verge of really serious trouble?

CURTIS: 'Cause we usually are. Goes with the job.

GIL: If I were you, I'd look at the map again. Although it won't do any good.

CURTIS: (*Studying the map.*) I'd say we're either over here: or over there.

GIL: Thank you. I have such an appalling rush of clarity, I could weep. So we could be one side of the border or the other. I'm so relieved that if I don't have to do anything urgent in the next couple of hours, I could happily spend the time taking your skin off.

CURTIS: Then you'd have no-one to tell you where you were. We could have stayed in that inn, if you hadn't started up that wager to see who could best mimic the landlord.

GIL: I'd have won, too.

CURTIS: You can see why they call this place The Blacklands.

GIL: Did I tell you I was born and grew up here?

CURTIS: Several times. It explains a lot.

GIL: The place has got worse lately, of course. I don't recognize it myself.

CURTIS: That's the point of The Upstart sending us here. To find out how much worse; and possibilities of invasion. But if we're caught, at least I can say I'm just checking the accuracy of the map. What's your story?

GIL: I felt like a change.

CURTIS: A change from The Marches?

GIL: Yeh.

CURTIS: But you're a Marchman, now.

GIL: I'll tell 'em the truth, that one of the perks of my job is that I don't have to stay in the shutcunt place.

CURTIS: And that your job happens to be patrolling the borders for signs of a raid?

GIL: How do you plan to explain your interest in maps?

CURTIS: Ever since my first fuck on a tumulus, I've been obsessed with contours. C'mon.

(*Enter SHAMBOCK.*)

SHAMBOCK: Little boys lost, far from home, shining up your sorrows. Suppose I'd better bring you in alive. Are you going to make life interesting for me? (*He disarms them with ease.*)

CURTIS: He definitely wasn't on the map.

GIL: He doesn't look like one of my relatives, either. (*Snap blackout.*)

SCENE TWO

(*Music. Lights up on WYE, surrounded by MISTRAL (who wears an eye patch), LONGWORTH, VIXEN.*)

LONGWORTH: You have incurred our displeasure. You bring witches into disrepute.

WYE: Excuse me: I was under the impression that a witch was a woman who'd made a point of becoming disreputable particularly well. And always, because she'd had to.

LONGWORTH: So you have to do what you do?

WYE: I do what I will. 'Reputation' is a stamp of approval you receive for obeying man-made rules. Of course I'm disreputable, I need to be disreputable.

MISTRAL: Nevertheless, Wye, you HAVE disrupted our long-term plans.

WYE: Have I now.

LONGWORTH: You have... associated with mortal men.

WYE: Yes, you ought to try it sometime. It's a splendid way of weaving grace and havoc. I particularly enjoy the havoc, and then usually find the grace takes care of itself.

MISTRAL: You've never been so foolish as to fall in love on one of these escapades, then?

WYE: Oh, there's nothing wrong with love if you do it for the sake of argument. Pardon me, I'm beginning to wonder if I've turned up at the Parish Young Wives' Knitting Circle by mistake?

VIXEN: (*Laughs.*) Yes, this is the slyping smatter of a Skevington's daughter.

MISTRAL: Thank you, Vixen, for that characteristically helpful contribution.

VIXEN: Characteristical, that's me. Vexacious quick brown hex trumps over the hazy fog.

LONGWORTH: (*To VIXEN.*) You just don't care, do you? She was like this as an infant. In fact, I defy anyone to tell the difference.

VIXEN: Infant a my own now, plollopped out ter plunder.

LONGWORTH: And what can you expect, with a mother like that and the amount of discipline she can't imagine, let alone enforce?

VIXEN: I can imagine you a magma fulla maggots. Wye's a wild wincopipe with a long sleek body an' a leopard's laugh, and you're not.

MISTRAL: Longworth: (*Who is about to explode.*) bottle it. (*LONGWORTH turns, seethes, subsides, and re-emerges with a small bottle which she places before MISTRAL.*) Vixen, go off somewhere and be lascivious, or stay here and show your sisters that you might be good for something else, for once. I have summoned this convocation to review and appraise the conduct and progress of our young necromantic colleague, who first delved into our realm when she was seventeen. Without having migrated to spirit capacity or elemental time, she has now arrived at the mortal age of thirty, leaving murmurs of rancour in her wake.

WYE: Spare me your pristine chagrin, whack it across someone else.

MISTRAL: Yes, I daresay this sounds brittle to someone like you. But after all, you have been known to assist the designs of mortal men. Some would say, challenge them. Your insistence on sexually defiant attire, for example, seems an eccentric choice of 'working clothes'.

WYE: Oh yes, I was wondering when you'd get round to that. Look, it's an outfit that I dreamed up, literally. I tried it out and enjoyed it. It helps me feel powerful when I 'go to work', as you would call it...

VIXEN: You wincin' at the way she charcoals her eyes'n'titlets?

WYE: (*To VIXEN rather than MISTRAL.*) They used to throw things at me. The outfit says, I stand my ground and throw it all right back. At all of them.

MISTRAL: Your contrary and contradictory nature is even reported to have led you to forsake your calling and join a mortal man's bed, only to re-emerge and fight on both sides of the battle since which the Blacklands have languished.

WYE: Yes, well, that's a long story, which I doubt whether you'd have time for.

VIXEN: What's wrong with Wye's waverings, or a good wanton wallow? (*She begins masturbating cheerfully.*) I like to lep a lumpkin an' drain out his drum, sap his spunk and his spit and what's left of his wit, sump his blood an' his gristle, make his pizzle a whistle, suck the flesh off his fingers whilst his eye-light still lingers, sink my teeth in his heart, give a volcanic fart, then I gnaw off the meat from what's shaken apart. That's a Vixen's licking.

LONGWORTH: Fascinating. Mind you, look what one of those forays landed you with.

VIXEN: My swippling son. Churning wamble brambling in the belly, rolling around in a sac of my kelp, knotting itself and myself into fat sweet fruit, then a fisting fish, webby ball bursting out of me for us to lap at each other. When I'd bit through the cord an' chewed up the blood-cake, I found I couldn't eat him after all. Other flesh droplets I'd chucked out my cunt, came out not done up right in the middle, so I'd shoved 'em back in the other end, scrunched 'em up in my teeth like baby birds, swallowed down all their gobby lumps, to curve back up through my bones and start back on the prowl.

LONGWORTH, WYE & MISTRAL: Yuk.

VIXEN: Surly slouching Shambock out from me on the prowl, too, tips life over and twists the head off it. Topples, breaks, sucks and chomps at the whole world. I turn him out from cluttering my cave, clambering all over my tasty space and belly time. He goes kicks holes in other things, an' chews their edges, with lovely greed. I let him. Vixen's got her own meat to sniff for.

MISTRAL: Which goes to prove that even a fiercely wayward spirit like Vixen cannot protect herself from all the consequences of ill-advised contact. And I carry my own inflicted reminder of a spurned offer, and its acrimonious wake (*Her eye patch.*). We think you must take care, my dear.

WYE: That's hutfucker policy. 'Take Care' with you everywhere at all times, lumber it onto other people, but never unburden yourself. Imagination only permitted in the cause of fear! What if there might even be a good cause in which to lose an eye?

MISTRAL: THIS WAS A GOOD CAUSE. I had silently protected a man for many years, but when I spoke my watchfulness and offered myself, he refused to trust himself to a woman's provision. Having nurtured this arrogance, I vowed that I would thereafter appear in many forms, at his moments of severest danger, to fight against him. I did so, then one day he did this, and broke free of me.

WYE: So you're a bad judge of men.

MISTRAL: Can you say with certainty that you have always judged them better?

WYE: Still have both eyes in. I didn't want to have to say that, Mistral, but if you back me into a corner, I tend to kick down the walls. Can't stand pre-emptive prescriptions, presumptions, preconditions or prigs: people who know they're right.

VIXEN: Wye's right. And she knows it!

WYE: People in flight from appetite.

MISTRAL: Shall I lift up this patch and show you what a man had an 'appetite' to do to me? (*Pause.*)

LONGWORTH: You go too far, Wye.

WYE: That's my speciality, kiddywink. (*LONGWORTH goes to MISTRAL.*) Alright, let me guess. You've summoned me here because you've thought of a way that I could repair this 'displeasure' I've 'incurred', by doing something you want me to. Apart from misguiding and admitting those two Marchmen into what is, from their point of view, the wrong part of the forest.

MISTRAL: Yes, this is an occasion on which you could assist, rather than ignore or obstruct, our designs. You may want our protection someday.

WYE: Protection from your designs, perhaps.

MISTRAL: Who knows? The Blacklands are proud but withering under the weight of conflict with their neighbouring land, the Marches. The ruler of the Marches, known as the Upstart, seeks alliance with us. If we agree, the independence of our power will pass to him. And then, it might be argued, our days as witches end.

VIXEN: Vixen never ends anything. I eat it all twice.

MISTRAL: Nothing lasts forever, Vixen -

VIXEN: - not even Nothing -

MISTRAL: - and as our power must eventually pass, to the envy of a stronger enemy, or to the tiredness spread by time, we would prefer to state a preference. We propose to make alliance with his rival, Empress Belia of the Blacklands.

WYE: Lucky girl. Maybe she'll gaze at you adoringly from time to time.

LONGWORTH: I'd say you're the one to tell us that. 'Old friend' of yours.

MISTRAL: Belia is a notable woman. Formidable, not least in her aspect. Her face and body were also harrowed up by men: a father who leased her out for usage, then visited his own mixed wrath and lust upon her; and a husband, to whom she was sold; who explored inside her, torturingly. However, she remade herself, an avenger of her life, and all such women's. Through stealth and strategy, she tricked the former King of Britain into giving her access to his court, to which she had also brought her father and husband, having tricked them into imprisonment. There, she ministered out her anger, and gravely wrought out from them a wash of blood to match her every tear. When the King fell, through some mysterious accident doubtless triggered by his own rash fecklessness, Belia's awesome just severity made her a magnet for similarly shackled and squandered womenfolk. Discovering her natural command of their unflinching loyalty and love, she accepted the invitation to preside over the Blacklands.

WYE: Who told you this story?

MISTRAL: It is a well-documented report of popular renown. And spiritual restorative.

LONGWORTH: Inevitably, the chronicles in the Marches tell a rather more reactionary version. And they refuse to acknowledge the name she gave herself. Instead, they hark back tauntingly to her father's fearful sneer of a name for her -

LONGWORTH & WYE: Wrayburn.

MISTRAL: You see: as Longworth claimed, she is known to you. And we predict she would respect your presence and heed your word, as our ambassadress.

WYE: I'm not sure. It's been three or four years since we met a couple of times. She wasn't that ready to listen to me, or to anyone else. Why not send Longworth, who could fail to like her or find her riveting...

MISTRAL: We have faith in your abilities to gain audience, to infiltrate and emerge from her fortifications safely, and to convey the gravity of our offer, in terms which she will weigh with respect. We would have no objection to your taking Vixen along, for company and protection, but you might well find her rather too - high-spirited.

WYE: I'll cope by myself, thanks very much.

LONGWORTH: We anticipated you would try to.

VIXEN: I'll spring along when there are arses for biting, testicles to be tasted, an' if it's women, I'll squat on their bellies an' let 'em look whilst I bring their breasts off bite by bite.

LONGWORTH: Honestly, Vixen, you are so - unfocussed.

VIXEN: Or a child in its cradle, cryin' ter mam. I slink in with the dark, pop up as Newblack Snoutymam, come ter sing an' nibble you awake, 'fore I snap off your head.

WYE: Does Vixen also cause problems for your 'reputations'?

MISTRAL: We ensure she's fed and exercised regularly, to minimize the outbreak of regrettable incidents.

WYE: I think I'll go now.

MISTRAL: Longworth will brief you as to your destination and message (*To LONGWORTH.*) Perhaps you could also point Vixen in the direction of a few particularly stupid sheep, on the way.

LONGWORTH: Certainly. (*She exits with WYE & VIXEN.*)

MISTRAL: (*Alone.*) And so, the divestment begins. Myself, into witch no longer, but - what? A one-eyed woman, staring holes in the dark. But knowing that the power has been placed aright. For a future, which I cannot be part of. Is that what they call 'peace'?

(*Fade to black.*)

SCENE THREE

(*Outskirts of a settlement: edge of darkness.*)

SHAMBOCK: Hey Mam! I wake up in the dark, an' the dark sticks to me. I get up and make myself do the same things, shit out shit and wet my head and shake the dark away. But you're still out there someway further; you lope and snarl, and I wait for something. You're butting the rushes to moisten your maw, and I'm inside the long wait of dried hide, stretching and creaking to whip. I hold back, 'cos I want something to let me touch everything. You stay out there to lick and bite, huggin' the night sky into you. I came in but I don't know why, so maybe it was right. Maybe it was him in me, tellin' me. I can't know, Mam, till you tell me who my dad was. I need to know what it is in me that's him, an' what's you, an' then what must be myself.

VIXEN: (*Leaping on his back and wrapping herself around him.*) Scrap a' skin on a kite of bones, same as any man.

SHAMBOCK: But you and him made me out a' nothin', an' it took your belly some time an' care to put all the nothin' together, so's you could send me out strong. Strong ter do what?

VIXEN: Whatever you like, trouble.

SHAMBOCK: What did he do?

VIXEN: Chuck his best bit of hisself into me.

SHAMBOCK: Why'd you let him?

91

VIXEN: Had an itch to stretch inside me a rooting skinpole.

SHAMBOCK: Why'd you pick him? 'Stead of another?

VIXEN: He'd gone apart from the others.

SHAMBOCK: An' how'd you know it was the best bit? It coulda' been his worst.

VIXEN: I sucks out their deepest cream when I fox men up. That's their good an' their dark all mixed up hard together into shiny bladderwrack butter.

SHAMBOCK: Right, Mam, I'll go on what you say, there. So what brought me in, to Them as lights fires against the dark? You say me dad strayed away from the fire, lookin' fer somethin' in the dark. It turned into you, an' wrapped itself around and straddled him. But what am I tryin' ter find in the light?

VIXEN: The light only shows 'em what they can buy, an' turn it all ter worry.

SHAMBOCK: I don't need light ter see my worry. Belia's bitches reckoned I was all their worries rolled inter one when I come out o' the dark at them on the Beltane night: no flames could keep me back. When I didn't bust 'em to bits, they were flummoxed.

VIXEN: I were, too.

SHAMBOCK: Got to find out why things are, where I am. Belia asks me in as her army pet, but soldierin's a long streak o' shite. If you feel good, you feel ricocheted an' mirrored up off others' faces; but if you get opencracked then everyone smells each other's blood, an' it runs out faster in fear.

VIXEN: Same as ever, bloodred roses, starin' dumb an' unbelievin' at the sprightly apartness places they'm broken into for the howlin' hwyl of it.

SHAMBOCK: Yea but, Mam. I'm shat out with me eyes left in. I know the trick now. I had to find out why, an' now I know. They don't let you out, from an army, from a country, 'cos it'd be a sign o' their own failure. If I don't wanna be all they say a man's good for - notwithstandin' the fact that I can be lowdamned good at it - that shows there's somethin' wrong wi' what they can offer. I'm lookin' at what they're offerin', but it ain't bought me or made me. If they can't offer better, I'm comin' back out ter the dark. But there must be somethin' here, 'cos me dad wanted somethin' from in here as well as somethin' from out there.

VIXEN: Per'aps 'e was just sackless saft.

SHAMBOCK: Per'aps. Then that's part of me too. But I'll come through: fox in me ain't trapshut in. Anythin' tries to claim me, even you Mam, I'll fract the rocks down on 'em.

VIXEN: (*Hissing fiercely.*) Yer a manky misbegotten marmaluke mongrel, an' that's that.

SHAMBOCK: (*Grabs her & stares into her.*) I know it, Mam. An' I know what you do, an' what that makes you. (*She starts to laugh; he joins in, then stops, and disentangles himself from her.*) An' one day there'll be nobody inside me but meself.

(*He stalks out; she glares after him and scurries away elsewhere. Fade to black.*)

ACT TWO, SCENE ONE

(*Belia's court. She is enthroned and flanked by SHAMBOCK & a GUARD, faced by GIL & CURTIS in chains.*)

WRAYBURN: Cartographers my arse. Hasn't word filtered back to you yet? We immediately know which interlopers are secretly Marchmen because they all say they're working on maps; their superiors are too stupid to have suggested that they use a different story.

GIL: Well, that's just him (*CURTIS*). I couldn't read a map if you paid me. I research - something else.

WRAYBURN: What?

GIL: (*Slightest pause.*) Sexual fantasies and practises. How they vary from one part of the land, to another. It's a topic everyone is bound to be interested in to some extent -

WRAYBURN: I'm not.

GIL: I've only just decided to begin collecting information, but I thought I'd start here.

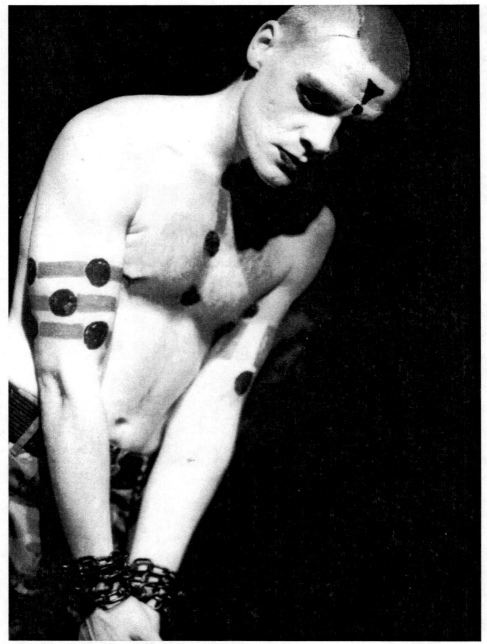

Rob Dean (Gil) in The Battle of the Crows.
Photo: Keith Morris.

WRAYBURN:	Why?

GIL: Well, it is the closest place to - yes, I'll admit it, the Marches, that's where we come from, but I myself was actually born here. Did you know the blacksmith who worked in the town just north of here fifty years ago?

WRAYBURN: No.

GIL: He was my grandfather. Did you know the town midwife?

WRAYBURN: Yes.

GIL: My grandmother was her two hundredth customer.

WRAYBURN: I'd say you were in training to become a village idiot, until your lack of progress and aptitude made them decide to send you here as a spy instead.

GIL: In my line of work, you begin to develop a surprising sense of hope in yourself. And appreciation of others. It's astonishingly rewarding, I can tell you. For example, your large friend here, (*SHAMBOCK.*) what does he do to - relax?

WRAYBURN: Dismemberment and appalling mutilation of people who talk too much. His name is Shambock, but his official title is The Claw: warning system, deterrent and executioner in one feral form. You obligingly strolled right up to him.

SHAMBOCK: Dull catch. Did't break a sweat.

WRAYBURN: One might even think that you were intended to provide a diversion away from some more artful form of transgression. (*Enter WYE.*)

WYE: Now, what girl could resist an entrance line like that? Remember me, Wrayburn? Sorry, Belia. How's the artful cutter?

SHAMBOCK: In here, undetected? You a cunning woman?

WYE: I go one better, bucko, I'm a witch. But, for once, I'm here to speak on behalf of those who would call themselves my sisters in magic. You and your cause are preferred, Belia. I've come to offer you help.

WRAYBURN: Really? Now, when I was a girl, I learnt three things. One: never require or rely on anyone's help. Two: never let yourself be taken off guard. (*She gives a sign to SHAMBOCK, who pinions WYE's arms. WRAYBURN removes WYE's necklace.*) Three: assume all initiatives from others to be hostile, eventually. Oh, I should now add number four. The witch called Wye has to wear her precious necklace in order to work her magic. Without it, she's as vulnerable and isolated as any woman.

WYE: 'Any woman' who's being needlessly manhandled? I really expected better from YOU, Wrayburn -

WRAYBURN: You're like the rest of them. You think you know best. I lead my own life now; with those who want to live similarly: on their own terms, and not meddled with. Chain her up, Shambock.

WYE: Vixen's brat?

WRAYBURN: He serves our purposes, in exchange for certain - liberties.

SHAMBOCK: I look, and I learn. (*Shackles WYE.*)

WYE: You never used to rely on a man to do your messy work for you.

WRAYBURN: There are some things which an Empress should not have to do, personally. Those loyal to her, will oblige.

WYE: You're just presuming hostility in everyone and everything.

WRAYBURN: Not always. But I judge when I can count on people, and when not. I'll book you in for a substantial, thoroughgoing introductory session of excruciating pain and permanent disfigurement with our talented resident torturer: but you'll have to wait a day or two before answering questions. When you find the proper staff, you have to offer them the opportunities to develop their skills. By the way, the guards on the door will be ordered and determined to keep you alive. They don't like to be deprived of their off-duty entertainment. (*She exits, with SHAMBOCK.*)

CURTIS: Is it your fault we fetched up here?

WYE: Someone told me to divert your path, I didn't know how this would develop. I'm not overjoyed about my own present situation, as you may possibly imagine.

GIL: I'd have preferred the idea that you acted out of spite. Instead, I'm facing the prospect of having my life ruined forever because you were doing what someone in charge told you to do. You deserve the worst that can be done to you, and I'm only sorry I won't have the chance to see it.

WYE: Excite you, would it? You're no better than these guards. But why should I expect anything different from a spy, ordered to uphold the pathetic little advantage that might belong to his land through slavishness to its law.

GIL: Who are you calling 'slavish'?

WYE: I've never liked Marchmen, probably because I don't understand them. Well, I can understand them insofar as I can tell what they're going to do next, which is very little. I don't respect them. They always want to split themselves off, somewhere down the line. They have no appetite to follow things through. They prefer to be ironic, because they're scared. And if they're too scared to be ironic, they set themselves up as 'lawmen', patrollers of the boundaries they've imposed on themselves and others.

GIL: He and I don't make laws or boundaries -

WYE: No, you just claim your importance and make your money from what you can stop people doing, in order to keep things as they are. Policing other people because you're afraid of yourselves. Justifying your existence at other people's expense. But that's the logical conclusion of what you understand by 'Englishness'.

GIL: So what makes you so much better than us?

WYE: I never sell myself short, and I always pay my way, somehow or other. There's nothing you can take from me in the name of 'the law'. I see I'm wasting my breath talking to you. But then, sometimes wasting things is fun. No, fun's the wrong word, I mean enjoyable and splendid. Not that I find talking to you either enjoyable or splendid. Would you possibly do me one favour, please? Would you fuck off and die? GUARD! Take me out of his sight! (*She stalks off accompanied by GUARD.*)

CURTIS: (*After a moment's contemplating GIL's dumb fury.*) Deep down, I'd say you and she quite like each other. (*Fade to black.*)

SCENE TWO

(Elsewhere in WRAYBURN's castle: ECHTERNACHT is whittling and sculpting a piece of wood, absorbed in his task. Enter WRAYBURN. She clears her throat. After a pause, she speaks.)

WRAYBURN: Oh good, you are in. Not that I'm particularly pleased to see you, of course. After all, the room is kept for you to come and go as you please, not as I. Why are you here today? Because of a piece of wood, evidently. Well, we all have our.
You'll never guess who turned up today. (*Inordinate silence.*)
Alright, perhaps you would.
Are you trying to?
Well, anyway, it's Wye. Reduced to broomsticking messages for the local chapter of hags. Amazing what we all come down to. (*Silence.*)
Yes I know, it's not amazing and you haven't come down to. You're well on with your continuing project of being the most irritating and inscrutable man alive. Not only irritatingly inscrutable; but also inscrutably irritating; you refine the distinction and, I believe, use it to cram the grey steel lantern jaws of your BLOATED PRIDE. I know you do, I can tell you. So. I could give the order for her to suffer terribly, you know. Wye, I mean. And have her beauty SHREDDED INTO TATTERS FOREVER. Well, I say forever, knowing her she could probably put it all back together again if she recovered her necklace, which is why she shouldn't. (*She hides WYE's necklace somewhere, unseen by ECHTERNACHT.*) Many people would thank me for ensuring that she shouldn't, not all of them women.

ECHTERNACHT: 'Shouldn't' or 'didn't'? And if many people were to thank you, so what?

WRAYBURN: SHUT UP. I mean, carry on. I mean, what do you mean?

ECHTERNACHT: Just what I say.

WRAYBURN: YOU ARE SO

ECHTERNACHT: I'm glad you find me so. How are you today?

WRAYBURN: Weary of people. You don't count, you're a monster.

ECHTERNACHT: (*Cheerfully.*) Thank you.

WRAYBURN: A self-created monster of egoism and aloofness and snobbery.

ECHTERNACHT: Danke schön.

WRAYBURN: And clinically insane.

ECHTERNACHT: I would hope so, by now. I do my best.

WRAYBURN: Have you any idea what a woman in my position risks by even
             wanting to talk to you?

ECHTERNACHT: Everything, I would hope.

WRAYBURN: And yet I do. Sometimes the only reason I try to find you is to try to
             find out why I try to find you. And I never do. I hate familiarity, so it
             can't be that.

ECHTERNACHT: And why do you try to find me today?

WRAYBURN: To confront something that makes my morality reflect upon itself.
             Which is evil, isn't it? You are a creature of the purest evil.

ECHTERNACHT: If you say so, then I am.

WRAYBURN: Sometimes I am so overwhelmingly glad I met you. Other days, I curse
             the very garments which could not hinder your conception. And
             wonder what they were.

ECHTERNACHT: Futile.

WRAYBURN: Yes. Kiss me. (*He does so.*) I am making a good job of everything. My
             subjects have never been more loyal, nor more loving. I find I cannot
             bear the presence of any one of them for more than a minute without
             screaming.

ECHTERNACHT: Perfectly natural.

WRAYBURN: I don't really want to have Wye tortured, she is so heartfelt and playful
             in her vanity. But then I find I do want her tortured to show that there
             are more powerful things than truth and wit.

ECHTERNACHT: And then what would you do?

WRAYBURN: Have myself tortured to be like her, of course. What do you think of my new costume?

ECHTERNACHT: It is an appalling enhancement.

WRAYBURN: Good, that's what I wanted. I developed the idea from her cruellest outfit. It's intended as an unforgettable simultaneous transfixion of my majesty and pain, intimating the unforgivable consequences of both.

ECHTERNACHT: It succeeds.

WRAYBURN: Good. Kiss me again. (*He does so.*) Right. Should I accept an offer of help from a witches' coven?

ECHTERNACHT: Find out why they want to give it.

WRAYBURN: Should I have two spies from the Marches put to death?

ECHTERNACHT: Find out why they want to live.

WRAYBURN: How should I do that?

ECHTERNACHT: Let me find out their greatest hopes, and their greatest fears.

WRAYBURN: Right. Thanks. I still love you, although I often wish you dead. But that is also futile, because you were not dead when I met you. And you are not dead when I meet you. And I have this grating horror that I might survive you.

ECHTERNACHT: You should try it.

WRAYBURN: You watch your back.

(*Fade to black.*)

SCENE THREE

(*Prison. GIL.*)

GIL: I hated her calling me a 'lawman'. It made me want to say, but that's only what I do. Sometimes. I resented the notion that I'd only made myself a man by maintaining the law. Or by maintaining anything. I wanted to tell her: they say I'm a sharp tactician because of my unpredictability. Others try to anticipate their opponents' moves, but I see what they're searching to turn themselves into. I can use what they want to be to stop them getting to it. She ought to respect that, because she does the same thing. I can tell. So. I'm clever because I can pre-empt others' actions. I do this in order to minimize their possibilities. I'm skilful because I can see their possibilities clearer than they can themselves, they are more scared of them than I am. I'm not scared of possibilities. I welcome them, and this helps me to be good at what I do. I glimpse possibilities in order to (*Pause.*) DIVERT them. I divert them so that I can (*Pause.*) win control. So that I am permitted to do anything. (*Pause.*) Who is permitting me? I am. So what do I do? I do not always maintain the law. Which is not to say that I break it. I choose not to. Why? Because that isn't how I wanted to make myself a man. Then how have I done it? By being quicker than the others. Quicker at what? Quicker at being them, and quicker at being myself. What is myself? It's all of my possibilities. I hate being underestimated. But that's how I win. Because I'm able to do things that they can't suspect I can. So why did I want her to know what I might be capable of? So that she can surprise me? No: so that I can surprise her. So that I can win. So that I can choose how things go. So that they stay as they are - no, I don't want that. I get angry with the way things are. I get angry with people who break the law. I get angry with the law, because people break it. I get angry because it makes them break it. I get angry. (*Pause.*) She made me angry.

(*Elsewhere: CURTIS.*)

CURTIS: I wonder how far away they've put Gil? Typical of him to make that outburst. Useful in a scrap, general good crack and often a stupid tosser. Somehow he thinks that by screwing up everything for himself and for everyone in the vicinity he's more alive than anyone else. Piercing capacity for insight into others, totally unmatched by any corresponding faculty for personal consideration or discipline. And that's because he's jealous of everyone: those who are more settled than him, those who are less settled than him, those who are richer, those who are poorer, those who are happier, those who are more miserable. And I've saved his neck and he's saved mine and it's typical of ME that I'm worrying about HIM. HE won't be worrying about ME. He's jealous of me, too. Of my wife, my home, my family. Of my knowing why I do the job: it's to protect them. I've tried to include him in our family, but you can't rely on him in that sort of way. Still, I admit, he makes me laugh, he makes me think, and we never fancy the same women. And I'm glad he's jealous of me. Because, sometimes, I am of him. I'm thinking about him to stop thinking about my wife and kids. My worst fear, after something terrible happening to them, is something terrible happening to me, and them finding out. Particularly if it wasn't a quick, clean death. I'd want them to remember, not HOW I died, but WHY. That's the witch's name. That they took prisoner. How does she fit in to this? If she's Wrayburn's enemy, is she our friend? She doesn't look like your standard Blackland harpy. It seemed so clear when the Upstart gave me the orders.

(*Flashback: lighting change: enter UPSTART.*)

UPSTART: To do the job well, you must know your purpose. So I meet my most significant men personally.

CURTIS: It's an honour, sire.

UPSTART: I dare say, I'm even younger than you expected?

CURTIS: Yes, you are.

UPSTART: It's been a swift year of change. With greater change to come. I surprise myself, but then I must if I'm to correct the drift. Do you know what I mean, when I say the drift?

CURTIS: The Blacklands building up forces? Making forays 'cross the border?

UPSTART: Something worse than their army. More subtle invasion. I'm told you have children. Tell me, when you're in the middle of playing with them, and you watch them smile with a true glow of contentment, d'you find it hurts?

CURTIS: Hurts?

UPSTART: Yes. Hurts that they're bound to suffer. Hurts that they can't stay this pleased, this easy. Wouldn't you do anything in the world to let them know - only such happiness?

CURTIS: Yes.

UPSTART: So don't you occasionally wish you could suffocate them? In their sleep, in a hug? (*CURTIS shifts uncomfortably.*) Has it never crossed your mind? To save them from slavery and violation? So that the death which they, and all of us, must eventually know, be administered as an act of love?

CURTIS: I think such thoughts cross many minds. Brief shadows of fear.

UPSTART: Nothing brief in these reports I've been receiving. Tobias Bratchell throttles both his kids then puts them in the wine-press. We find him and his wife drinking their juices. 'Puttin' 'em back inside us to keep 'em safe', he explains. Gloria Trellis, village schoolma'am, waits till her parents deliver all the kids, then makes 'em line up so she can teach 'em silence with a knife. 'Despatched with grace', she tells those left mad with grief. Why now, so many?

CURTIS: Who can tell?

UPSTART: I must, if I'm to rule this land. And your wife, Curtis. When you hold her in the night. If we were invaded, she'd be chained, repeatedly raped, infected and literally defaced. We all know that. But something worse. Have you found yourself thinking: you'd do these things to her yourself? To prevent them being done by others? To place her, beyond their reach of filthy hungers?

CURTIS: No - I couldn't -

UPSTART: You'd find a cleaner way?

CURTIS: I'd try to think of one -

UPSTART: This is what I call the drift. A slow twisting, furring and ulcerating of people's inmost reachings, turning love to lesions. It's vile, it appals me, and I know it's on the increase from those who dare to report or confess it. I am glad for the courage they find to speak it, and for mine, to hear and answer it. Something's OUT THERE, Curtis: gradually turning us inside out to ourselves and those closest to us. It's witchcraft. That wretched Belia - Wrayburn of the Blacklands - is the source of it: so in love with her own scarred reflection that she want to disfigure us into her apes of pain. She's made some bargain with the dark. So what would you do if you were me?

CURTIS: I'd look to discover - and tackle - this business at source.

UPSTART: Exactly. And people may doubt my abilities, still. Who can blame them, I'm not fully a man, still short of my coming-of-age. Placed here by a popular groundswell I was too young to vote in. Nonetheless, Curtis, I hope to be a man, one day, in the fullest sense, like you. Else how can I know and rule other men with right? We must be determined, Curtis: to prove and show ourselves as men, unafraid: for the sake of other men and women, and the future.

CURTIS: I will.

UPSTART: But, even as you go to seek out this fear, be properly afraid, as I am. For everything tells me, Curtis: something is watching. Something which considers itself to be outside and above humanity. And therefore sees no reason to be stopped, by humanity. I do not know how to stop it. But I know that first we find it, and see its face. We must.

CURTIS: We will. (*Reverie of UPSTART vanishes.*) And if I can't do better than this, our time will run out. And it will only remain, for us to be the toys of something devilish. Worse, because nameless, and somehow already within...

(*Elsewhere: WYE.*)

WYE: Witches never last long after they're blinded or crippled or had their noses opened out, and that's just as well. But the mockery and the spite and the vengeful REFUSAL TO IMAGINE twists that time into an infinity of awfulness, that can piss on your every moment of pride and pleasure ever known. I either wanted to die so woundingly beautiful that people died in the stampede of pilgrims determined to fuck my corpse, even though they knew the glass coffin was unbreakable; or else to die so generously lined and elegantly haggard that exactly the same event occurred. Either way, I wanted a triumphantly artificial death, to reflect and crown my witchy life. Not butchered vulnerability, but of course Wrayburn knows all about that, abuses and their uses, and now she has some authority she helpfully wants to inflict it on those more fortunate than herself. Funny: I remember thinking after I'd watched her rake her husband's bits away to red blobby strings, here was a young woman of extraordinary promise and initiative. Now there she is, and here I am. Perhaps I don't want to die alone. Perhaps I want SOMEONE TO KISS ME AND KEEP ME THEIRS FOREVER, no, no, don't be silly, that's adolescent codswallop with roses and phials of poison round the door, that's preliminary fittings for matching marble slabs with fine print regarding simultaneous usage, EVERYBODY DIES ALONE YOU CLUELESS BINT, but I don't want pity or its refusal. Come on, Wye, you have to find a way to show yourself a jumping jezebel right to the end of the line.

(*A trap door opens. It is ECHTERNACHT.*)

ECHTERNACHT: You just did. Merci.

WYE: ECHTERNACHT! How did you get here?

ECHTERNACHT: In the wake of my own similar experiences, I persuaded Wrayburn to build a concealed exit from every cell, to reward the particularly resourceful and creative prisoner, or to permit moments of devastating empathy between gaolers and captives.

WYE: YOU BASTARD. THAT BITCH. So you've been TOYING with me by keeping me here. I've half a mind to INSIST on STAYING HERE, until I work out a way to escape myself. There's power for you, they even want to deprive you of the right to despair, and the shocking bolts of perception that you can find on its other side.

ECHTERNACHT: Do you want to prowl around developing aphorisms, or do you want to escape?

WYE: What about my necklace?

ECHTERNACHT: Wrayburn has secreted it somewhere. I cannot locate it yet.

WYE: I can't leave without it.

ECHTERNACHT: Then face the torturer, without it. She cannot permit the disclosure that she permitted two enemy spies to go free, or that such a thing as a witch might exist to either advance or threaten her cause. You and the Marchmen must abscond covertly, and I am offering my unique manner of assistance.

WYE: Why?

ECHTERNACHT: Because once you offered to try my fears, to discover what was on the other side of me. Thus you helped me to find the right danger, in myself and others. Now let me extend your curiosity for the questionable and terrible.

WYE: (*Hesitating.*) Are you in league with Wrayburn?

ECHTERNACHT: Can you honestly imagine me in league with anybody, even myself? Your wits are glib and blunted, Wye. Once you acted like an elemental force, ageless and exploratory. Deprived of your necklace, you are a skittish colt of a girl again. I preferred the more commanding performance.

WYE: And the Echternacht I knew would never gloat.

ECHTERNACHT: You are right, I demean myself: thank you for the observation. No,

Wrayburn and I spent some time in examination of our lives, the world and each other: then our ways diverged: she searched out and protected women who had suffered similarly to herself, and then was elevated by them and others towards greater powers. I tended increasingly towards a solitary contemplation. It is thought injurious for her to acknowledge me as a former consort, but we still manage the odd clandestine tryst of mutual offence and grudging fondness. It is surprising, really, but that is why we persist in it. And sometimes, such as now, I go about the business that she intends but prefers not to admit. In return, she slyly gives me food, shelter and a splendid harpsichord. Now, let us collect your fellow prisoners and I will escort you back to the border. Can you contact your coven from there?

WYE: I - don't know. Without my necklace, I'll have to wait for them to contact me.

ECHTERNACHT: Astride power's capricious blade! But so it is for us all. Come along, quickly. (*They exit & lights fade.*)

SCENE FOUR

(*The Marches. Torchlit hubbub. One speaks.*)

UPSTART: Brave neighbours: it appears that the renowned bogland wildcat has a worse shape than legend could suggest. Apprehended on the hill, strayed over from the Blacklands no doubt, the direst travesty she-beast ever to hatch from woman's conjurings: look at it, and shrink from its filth. (*VIXEN is illuminated, in a cage.*) Our sentries found it treading a quagmire of sheep and men which had been shriven into jellied blood. As she lapped at her vile undoings, they sprang the net, then hauled her to this cage. Gaze on it: parody beast, parody woman, fit for neither, mocking both. And over the hill: black widow Belia, who would make your children thus misshapen and enslaved to their basest hungers, and her own. The time approaches to rescue these hideous hybrids from the pain and confusion of their inly riven selves, resolving them to beast or man or simple pure base matter, from which unspoilt life might spring.

(*Two crowd members turn: they are MISTRAL & LONGWORTH, in cloaks.*)

MISTRAL: Find her some particularly stupid sheep, I said.

LONGWORTH: These looked particularly stupid.

MISTRAL: Yes, but that was because they were farmers playing decoy in lumpy sheepskins, with painted marrows for muzzles. Really, Longworth, I know you're still only on probationary training, but when did you last see a sheep wearing boots?

LONGWORTH: Vixen didn't notice either. In fact, she remarked on how savoury they were.

MISTRAL: She would. The question now, is: how best to preserve dignity. I think you should leave this part to me.

LONGWORTH: You will be able to save Vixen, won't you? Even if we do call her The Embarrassment, I don't like the sound of those plans which the human beings have simmering for her.

MISTRAL: You're just ashamed of your part in this farrago. You'll know worse before you're much older. Now be off with you.

(*LONGWORTH exits, crestfallen; light change to the UPSTART's quarters, where he sits, and pours a drink. VIXEN's cage is placed upstage.*)

UPSTART: No use gnawing those bars, beastwench. We prepared them specially for you, too thick for your jaws to snap.

VIXEN: They'll provide me practice for your hip bone steaks. No one betters a witch come winter, bear-whelp.

UPSTART: I don't think you'll see winter, this year. I suppose if we put your bleached bones in a freakshow, they might twinge with the frost. Don't rely on much more. And a bear-whelp I may be; but I lick myself into my own shapes, quicker than a witch can follow.

MISTRAL: (*Coming forth.*) So why, I've often asked myself, would a young man of such ingenious attack embrace and retain the name 'The Upstart'? It hardly does credit to your eloquence and presence.

UPSTART: And for what, I ask myself, did the forward but comely lady forsake an eye?

MISTRAL: For failing to realize where I might best be appreciated. Cruel joke, from a man I had invited to look into me.

UPSTART: Cruel indeed. And now I'll answer you: I help the people feel superior to what they want. Including me. They like the brash, youthful energy

107

of my plans and promises, and so join in my schemes even as they smile at them; no doubt they debate my shortcomings long into the tavern nights: 'He's young, he'll learn; he'll change, like all of us'. But no one can specify what I am to learn, should you put them to it. I offer them a share in a young man's heyday; they think I'll pay the piper, and not them. When all along it's me that plays the tune.

MISTRAL: That sounds precocious, but also vacuous.

UPSTART: Yourself, for example. You think yourself branded into consequences by your injury and your maturity. But you could make of them what you wish. Perhaps that man struck out your eye out of shame, enraged by recognition of a love which he could never equal, and set you wandering beyond him, for a time and place where a beauty that exceeds symmetry would be justly hailed, and might drive others to spurn an eye for fashion.

MISTRAL: As flatterers go, you're not the worst that I've encountered.

UPSTART: Nor are you.

MISTRAL: The 'beastwench', as you call her. She is a sort of sister-liability to me. She galls me, but I would not forsake her.

UPSTART: Strange family, to breed such a sister.

MISTRAL: From an arcane outreach. What's your price, to set her free?

UPSTART: There may not be one. I could use her autopsy to prove Belia's nightmarish degenerations, and rouse the Marchmen against the Blacklanders once and for all. Or else: I may set her free forever, to show amity with her sister and the order of beings she represents. For whilst demonesses may be chased and hounded down over the border, I might discover and demonstrate the existence of good guiding spirits on this, our side of the soil, joining and urging us on.

MISTRAL: I see. An ultimatum, in the package of a bargain. You overestimate Vixen's importance to me: I am not prepared to sell myself into slavery. She can be a hostage to be associated with our more drastic actions, and their unpalatable extremity will naturally die with her, rogue unrepresentative creature that she is.

(*VIXEN hears and reacts to this.*)

UPSTART: I'm not proposing anything so monotonous as slavery. Why seek to shame the shameless? I find your power deeply impressive, and would prefer to show you how I might serve it.

MISTRAL: Serve us?

UPSTART: Serve you. You see, I have never fully known a woman. I lost my mother years ago, under terrible circumstances. No sister, nor ever a young woman friend. Whilst there's much that I know, there's much that I WOULD know: you, as deeply as you'll let me.

MISTRAL: I fear not.

UPSTART: 'Fear', indeed. What have you to lose, from my offer of myself? Will you sentence me to never be a man? For all my swift achievements, I know that's the taunt they make behind my back.

MISTRAL: Sorry, I'm not a devirginating contraption -

UPSTART: And I'm not seeking a password which enables me to rule a coven but leaves me as alone as ever. Would you prefer to remain superior to me? I think we are rather alike: porcelain monuments to ourselves, aloof, apart and alone. But when I look into your eyes, I wonder whether I have tried too hard to protect myself from some forces. Though even if you were to - give yourself away to me - you might find me out to be more boy-actor than monarch; or man, even. I might have to ask you to show some patience while I learn best how to - love every part of you as it - as you want, and deserve. I know, I can't be your first - but you might also discover some newness in yourself, with me -

MISTRAL: (*Breaking an increasingly engulfing contact.*) What net are you trying to throw over ME?

UPSTART: Come back, tomorrow, and I'll set her free, no matter what you say, I promise. Just give yourself a chance to think about what I've said. Please don't recoil away from me so quickly, forever: that's all.

MISTRAL: (*Pause.*) Tomorrow.

UPSTART: Yes. (*MISTRAL leaves.*) To all it holds. (*Drain his glass and exits, leaving.*)

VIXEN: So the Upstart's a vengeling with an itchy cock to crow up some crevice. But that Mistral would strand a Vixen in an urgin' virgin's vaults so they could tar her with trespasses so's theirs is the kingdom, smart an' deadquick! An' then have me filletted for a freakshow? If I can spring out of this hutch, I'll dig up some bones to leave at their door. But I'm fixed here, fast as a fist up a ferret's arse! I'll dream of things, I'll do to 'em all.

(*Lights fade.*)

ACT THREE, SCENE ONE

(*In the wilderness: ECHTERNACHT leads on GIL, CURTIS & WYE.*)

CURTIS: Are you sure you know where the border is?

ECHTERNACHT: Of course I know where the border is! I just don't know what direction I'm going in.

GIL: That makes me feel much better.

WYE: Suits me fine. As long as it's away from there.

ECHTERNACHT: Enjoy the bleakness!

(*Enter Two Soldiers.*)

1st SOLDIER: Oi. Are you Marchmen or Blacklanders?

ECHTERNACHT: Do I look or sound like either? Once I was a German mercenary, fighting for the French army, until I was stranded here. Ever since, I follow my own course, and wish you good fortune in doing the same.

2nd SOLDIER: But where are you going?

ECHTERNACHT: Wherever we can.

2nd SOLDIER: What for?

GIL: To get away from stupid questions.

1st SOLDIER: Hey now, that's not a stupid question. That's duty. And so is this. (*He hits ECHTERNACHT, who doubles up.*) And we could decide that cutting your tongue out was, as well.

2nd SOLDIER: Or making you cut out your friend's tongue. Or your woman's.

GIL: She's not actually 'mine'. Or any one's.

1st SOLDIER: Then I'm almost tempted to say you could join in the fun and games after we've finished with 'er, if you're so inclined. But I have this thing about foreigners (*ECHTERNACHT cries out as 1st SOLDIER stands on his hand*.). And that includes people looking for the border, who aren't patrolling this side of it, like us.

GIL: (*To WYE.*) Enlightened regime your friend runs, isn't it? Good to see how thoroughly her views on abolishing victimization have permeated the ranks.

CURTIS: Come on, lads. Let us go on our way, and where's the hassle?

GIL: Oh, here. Here's the hassle. (*Very fast:*) Right then, me merry Union Blackjacks, let's be having you. I mean, really having you. Really reaching inside what makes you want to use a Marchman's brains for boot dubbin, well it can't be the wages or the fringe benefits so I suppose it must be to do with feeling that little bit better, in your skin, when you prove you're in the best place and they're in the worse, which they certainly are when you're standing there together scouring the floor with their faces. In fact, yes, I see the error of my ways, move over, I'm joining up.

1st SOLDIER: Eh?

GIL: Yes, I want to join you, like you, be like you and even, whisper it quietly, love you in that forthright, sparring, bluff, stolid, affectionate, reliable way that we lads have.

2nd SOLDIER: You want to what?

GIL: Give you a hand here in leaving these greasy dregs just twitchingly alive enough for them to crawl back home and plaintively waggle their stumps at their nearest dearest rank'n'filibusters till they gasp and whisper at the full uncoiled magnificence of our lashing disdain.

CURTIS: (*To WYE.*) It's all right. This is what he does.

GIL: Take, for example, the slack old wretches who say 'It's all right. This is what he does'. They think that you're limited by your acts and decisions, it never occurring to them that it's their lack of any significant act or decision that makes you have to do things, like pointing out that their SMITHEREEN DIGNITY is made up of cobwebs stringing together the things they prefer NOT TO DO. And why's he made himself like this? For a wife and kids somewhere, a wee wifey and romping sprogs using the hearthrug for a snotrag while the kitchen fills with the gentle aroma of baking cakes, blocked drains and burning thatch, but then you see that's what makes a man a man, his ability to stand aside and let other people do things in his name (like walk all over him and keep him grindingly poor, for example) while he looks on with generosity, equanimity and poise. So let's put that poise to the test, boys, it's what he's been waiting for. Hang on! Lord love a lumpfish, it IS what he's been waiting for. Yes, he WANTS to be the pitiful martyr who one day just effaced the blood clean out of his veins, with a touch of expert help from us, giving up what he had, somewhere else apart from wherever those he chose to die for actually happened to be, well, they're never going to forget or stop feeling morally inferior to THAT then are they, they're never going to have to smell him reeking of booze and stealthy decay as he contemplates what's left in life, a parade of opportunities to be increasingly boring to others and himself and to glimpse the rising tide of DISGUST in their eyes, no sirree, he'll ascend on high into clouds of remembered glory while they slowly but precisely whittle themselves away under the strain of trying to work off the moral debt, the ever-receding smug fat sallow titty of ATONEMENT that they too will cut their balls off to try and suck. Whoops, wait a minute, better not let him think too much about that, he might change his mind. No, sorry, he doesn't have a mind left to change, he swapped it for a sense of duty, not the same sort of duty as you lads cuddle up to of course, perish the thoughtbox, no his own sort of inbred slackjawed gormless sadeyed dopeygrinning MARCHMAN sort of duty, different sort of zebra I assure you. Now what about over here? (*ECHTERNACHT.*)

2nd SOLDIER: Well, he's definitely a foreigner.

GIL: Give that man a string for his Wooden Duck. Yes, he's definitely a foreigner, and not only that but he's a particularly slyly THIN sort of foreigner as if he can only bear to let his precious white aristocratic skin brush up against the bare minimum of air it has to slide through, whilst carefully averting the genteel nostrils and proud brow from the presence of cowpats like us. Though come to think of it, giving him a good kicking would actually satisfy him in his heart of hearts. Look into his eyes: this man wants to be given things that he can prove that he can RISE ABOVE. Are we going to play into his hands and give that to him? Are we fuck. So then.

1st SOLDIER: Hang on. She looks like she's planning something.

GIL: Well, I daresay she is. Milady Sphinx over here is all for planning how to make people try to guess what she's planning, and you can see by that arch of the neck but also that tilt of the chin how she's interested BUT ONLY SO INTERESTED as to put her hands on her hips (*WYE realizes she has put her hands on her hips, and drops them.*) to turn sideways and look somewhere to the left or right of you as if scanning the horizon for a REAL challenge. She thinks she makes things start. Let's prove otherwise. Let's make her make things - stop. Then we'll see what she does. (*Pause. All shift uncomfortably, except GIL.*) There you go, you see. We made her make NOTHING HAPPEN. That'll give her a thing or two to think about over the next few weeks, by jingo. She'll be checking that mirror and tapping the sides of it to knock out the blockages that must have built up. She won't forget us in a hurry, I can tell you. So, thank you, me jolly jack blacklads, it's been a good sprightly whack of a way to take the eyes and mind for a walk. I've learnt a thing or two, I can tell you. I don't yet know exactly what, but no doubt it'll jump up when it has to, and so may we all. Hey, you better take these with you (*GIL offers back the weapons he has stealthily removed from them during all this.*) - no telling what outlandish rascals you might run into. Step lightly, an' keep your woggles clean. (*SOLDIERS exit in a daze.*)

CURTIS: You had me worried for a minute there. But that was a fine performance.

GIL: It came easily. Probably because I meant every word of it.

CURTIS: Meaning what?

GIL: You can cross the border if you want to. I can't see the point.

CURTIS: You're staying here?

GIL: No, I'm NOT GOING BACK, there's a difference. You saw those blockheads? That's US. We patrolled borders, and made sneaky little trips over them. Perhaps you can still do it, you believe in things like safety and futures. I've decided they're ways to avoid the present.

WYE: So what do you want, then?

GIL: What do I want? I want us all to stop pretending that we're not going to DIE.

ECHTERNACHT: Of course we will die. That is a truism that only an adolescent vanity could parade as a revelation. The point is: to know why you die: for what purpose, on whose terms.

GIL: ALL RIGHT, I DON'T. I thought I did. So I have this talent, this facility, that people find useful, people more rich and powerful than me. I help them out, they toss me a few crumbs. But all I've done is keep things as they are. I look around, and I see that NOTHING I HAVE DONE HAS MADE A DIFFERENCE. NOT TRULY.

ECHTERNACHT: (*Pause.*) Once: I felt the same.

GIL: And now?

ECHTERNACHT: Now: I do not know.

GIL: And is that all you have to show for a life?

WYE: And what do you have?

GIL: Nothing. But at least I know it.

CURTIS: Easily said. Let's see you not having the warmth to sleep, or food.

GIL: So look around you. Look at this land. What 'difference' have you all made? Eh?

(*Silence. Slow fade.*)

SCENE TWO

(*Firelight. WYE & GIL awake; ECHTERNACHT & CURTIS asleep.*)

GIL: So what do you want?

WYE: I used to say: 'ways to abandon'. Ways to walk away. I'm a bit like him (*Touches ECHTERNACHT*). Finding out what I can step away from, free.

GIL: Alright, I've stepped. So now what do we do?

WYE: Never be caught.

GIL: Never?

WYE:	Not entirely.
GIL:	Irony.
WYE:	No.
GIL:	You can be caught, but only partially?
WYE:	Perhaps.
GIL:	No thanks. I'm sick of half measures, and dividing yourself up for others.
WYE:	Yes.
GIL:	What would you like?
WYE:	Nothing like anything.
GIL:	Where do you start?
WYE:	Wherever I am.
GIL:	Where do I start?
WYE:	Wherever you want.
GIL:	Good. (*He kisses her.*) Goodnight. (*He turns over and goes to sleep. She looks at him for a moment, then decides to do the same. Fade.*)

SCENE THREE

(*Lights up on MISTRAL.*)

MISTRAL: So what was I supposed to do? 'Prove your strength by holding back' said the mature, shrewd woman perfectly alone with her one keen eye. But I didn't want to face the rest of my life and memories alone with her. I find I can't. So yes, I told him. I dare not hold you. Let me hold you. Let's look and reach and touch inside each other too much. My lost eye has a brilliance for not seeing, so let's make the impossible necessary. But we did not rush. Let's make time an ally rather than a thief, I said. 'I said'. Who was this woman speaking her new voice through my old face? My remaining eye seemed more hers than mine.

I told her, 'Lend me the strength to be incapable of drawing wisdom's sad conclusions. Because, like them, we will fade soon enough'. What else could matter? And when I asked, 'Am I all you have in the world?', he laughed, and said 'Not quite'. He said that he had one relative left alive, out travelling with his associates. He placed his hand on my head, so when he asked me 'Bring them here', I did. (*An effect of sound and light. THE UPSTART appears alongside MISTRAL: so do ECHTERNACHT, CURTIS, GIL & WYE.*)

WYE: Mistral. You found me. But this isn't one of your places -

UPSTART: No, it's one of mine. (*To GIL & CURTIS.*) Welcome back, boys. You will understandably feel disorientated for a moment, although I gather Gil feels more substantially - displaced.

WYE: Mistral, why are you doing his bidding? You said we should offer our help to Wrayburn -

MISTRAL: I've stopped seeing inflexibility as a virtue, Wye. I'm convinced that this side can offer us more.

WYE: Or have you just stopped seeing? Except if we're bait on your line, useful only when hooked.

MISTRAL: How useful are you now, to anyone, without your necklace?

GIL: Who's the bitch with the patch?

CURTIS: I don't know, but I have a sick feeling we're in the wrong company.

UPSTART: Nonsense, Curtis. Mistral is my consort and partner in expanding the operation of the realm we love so much, and Wye is a formerly troublesome old acquaintance of hers. But the main purpose in bringing you here is to for me to see Echternacht. It's been many years.

ECHTERNACHT: You puzzle me. I cannot recall us ever meeting.

UPSTART: I'm disappointed. But someone else should also witness this reunion. (*He places his hand on MISTRAL's head, and WRAYBURN appears.*) Hello, you tawdry Amazon of misrule. Look what you've fallen into.

WRAYBURN: Oh no. Wye, this must be your doing, I knew you could never be trusted -

116

WYE: It's not my doing. I think the situation's much worse than my pranks ever permitted.

UPSTART: I'm about to deny you the satisfaction of believing that, Wye. I think it's time for me to tell everyone how, once upon a time, one of your 'pranks' involved sending a renegade soldier - an escaped prisoner - to the hovel of a family, who graciously offered him food and lodging. They trusted him, for all his truculence. The mother welcomed the opportunity to extend her benevolence. The father did his best to offer companionable support for a fellow who was experiencing poor fortune. The boy of the family saw him as another benign, if eccentric, presence. He graced the newcomer with the name of 'uncle'. All was well until one morning the boy awoke: he found his parents dead, and only his uncle remaining. When he asked what had happened, the uncle told him two stories. One, that the parents had elected to die quietly and to leave the house and patch of land for the boy to harvest alone. Two, that the parents became unaccountably seized by greed and determined to kill the boy, but the uncle intervened and saved him. The uncle told the boy to believe whichever story gave him the keenest resilience, courage and appetite for life. And then he stepped away, leaving the boy to find a way to survive alone. He justified this ABANDONMENT by claiming that it was an educative preparation for life, and the 'essential solitude' which we must all supposedly face.

WYE: Oh. Oh no. Echternacht: don't listen. He's not a real boy. HE'S NOT A REAL BOY!

UPSTART: (*To WYE.*) And why are you more real, you wanton broken wand? I would say the boy took this lesson to heart. No one ever stays here with you. It's wrong to expect it, or even to want it. I have manifested my courage, resilience and appetite by persuading people to let me take power, which certainly makes this 'essential solitude' much more enjoyable. You see, I decided that there was a third possibility: that you killed my parents, and left me stranded, out of jealousy for what we had. You could not share in it, however much we invited, so you had to destroy it, and leave my early life a wreckage. You hated our happiness because you felt superior to it, you broke our lives to prove your theories, you proposed an impossible ideal at the cost of my childhood, you adorned yourself in the fabric of pain torn from me, whom you so casually discarded.

ECHTERNACHT: Wait. That is not how your parents died. Let me tell you -

UPSTART: Oh, but you said I was to believe whatever made me stronger. I do.

117

Admit it, uncle. And admit your crimes. And welcome back. (*UPSTART puts one hand on ECHTERNACHT'S shoulder and casually plants a dagger in his breast with the other. ECHTERNACHT stares at it and gasps with surprise.*) Now, do you know what I call that? (*The dagger.*) I think it's 'essential solitude'. And this is your time to face it. Have the dignity to do so with some 'courage'. (*ECHTERNACHT buckles, falls dead.*) No-one ever stays here with you, after all.

WRAYBURN: (*Her voice finally breaking through her mounting horror.*) No. NO. NNOOO! (*She lets out an appalling wailing shriek of irrevocable loss.*)

(*Fade to black, and silence.*)

– INTERVAL –

ACT FOUR, SCENE ONE

(*The Blacklands: WRAYBURN, WYE.*)

WRAYBURN: I can't eat, I can't sleep, HE'S KILLED SO QUICKLY THE ONLY MAN I EVER LOVED. How could he - how could we let him - TAKE ECHTERNACHT AWAY FROM ME - AND FROM EVERYONE ELSE - FOREVER AND EVER? How could that grinning DEMON just - PLUCK AWAY - every possible thing that Echternacht could have done or said or felt for years and years to come? He has torn the heart out of my future, and I want to die too, except that my sweat keeps pumping out FROTHS OF RAGE at how casually he did it - and then how he could laugh at what he'd done, and at my grief - and turn us loose to come back here and try and live with what we'd seen, and what I know can never happen. All because of SOMETHING YOU ONCE DID?

WYE: Please listen. The Upstart's lying. Echternacht didn't kill his family -

WRAYBURN: WHO GAVE HIM THE POWER TO LIE? WHO GAVE HIM THE POWER TO MOVE?

WYE: What we call The Upstart - isn't human. Nor wicca. When I found Echternacht roaming the wilderness, I freed three spirits, confined to the limbo of the half-hearted. I made them enact a riddle for him, and had them assume the shapes of a mother, father and boy. They performed a vision: of life-in-death and death-in-life. Echternacht grasped the riddle and went beyond it, seeking to touch the boy into life as he went. And, in a terrible way, he did. The spirits who had played out the parts of mother and father were freed to dissolve away: the spirit who had assumed the boy's shape would not. He refused to release himself into the elements; but he would not follow Echternacht's drive into the face of the world; inwardly riven, like anything trying to be even partly human, he cannot make sense of his pain, and so blames it on the world he cannot fully enter - and on the man who made him want to enter it...

WRAYBURN: (*Bitterly.*) So it's true. Your meddling set free something that has laid my world to waste. Made it again, as it used to be. Before I met someone to give me hope that not all men - (*Sniffs, bracingly.*) not that he couldn't be a real pain in the arse like the rest of them, of course, very frequently he was. But his cruelties, to others and to himself, always had some larger purpose, often of strange irrational generosity.

So where am I to find generosity of purpose now? I have never known it elsewhere. Echternacht was evidently a ludicrously steadfast and clean aberration in a world arranged around a gradual but definite movement towards increasing IDIOTIC AWFULNESS. I suppose I must become an awful idiot, with the rest.

WYE: Then you will become another Upstart, if you refuse to let imagination shape your pain. And you will dishonour the soul of Echternacht, and your own.

WRAYBURN: WHAT DO YOU MEAN, SOUL? YOU'RE TALKING LIKE A DRUNKEN PRIEST.

WYE: Return my necklace.

WRAYBURN: No.

WYE: How else do you propose to make change? Through more destruction and injury?

WRAYBURN: Don't try to tell me that isn't what it usually entails.

WYE: I can't.

WRAYBURN: LIFE IS INJURY. All we can do, is try to make something out of it.

WYE: Yes. Just don't let it make something out of you.

WRAYBURN: GET OUT OF MY SIGHT BEFORE I BLIND YOU.

WYE: I belong nowhere, so I cannot be banished. My only place is just out of reach of whatever tries to control me, reject me, dismiss me or incorporate me. Attempt these things, and I will come down unbidden. Necklace or none.

WRAYBURN: Oh, Wye. (*WRAYBURN suddenly embraces her.*) And when I first stepped within reach of Echternacht - not knowing whether we would kill or kiss each other - you tried to stop me. Why was that?

WYE: Fear. Of the will to change. Don't congeal all your feelings into a headstone for a man, because he's died, Wrayburn. You'll fall in love with limits. Echternacht would not want that.

WRAYBURN: No.

WYE:　　　　　So let's find out. What happens after.

(*Lights fade.*)

SCENE TWO

(*The Marches: THE UPSTART's tower; he sits in contemplation. MISTRAL approaches him.*)

MISTRAL:　　　Our second night, my dark cold-handed boy. They say that the first time you kill a man, is a loss of one sort of virginity. You horrified me, stealing away his life, with your thief's hands. And now the thought excites me. That drastic, remorseless, irrevocable movement of your hands. I want them over me. Let them take away what they will. Let them give what they can. Let them find out, and so will I. I find, in myself, so much to give you. Please look into - my eye. Here. First skin I'll shed, is that of witch, so you'll be the first man to have me as a woman (*Places her hand on his forehead.*). My powers I'll freely give away to you, unasked. I'll be stripped of one witchery, and torn into another, placing my power in a future I'll be part of. To think I wanted peace: who could prefer it to this sick delicious raging of blood and skin's clamour? Take away my former power, and with it my old self (*Sound/lights suggest transfer of power from her to him.*). Now you will have whatever you want. And so will I. I want you to look here. (*She bares her breasts, and invites his gaze. She then turns and undresses completely. She steps out of her clothes, and presents her backside to him. She performs all these actions with exquisite precision.*). I want you to look here. (*She turns, naked except for eye patch, and faces him again. She kneels to a squat, opening her legs to him.*) I want you to look here. (*With ultimate abandon, she removes the eye patch.*) Look into me: then taste and touch my every depth. (*UPSTART falters; she voices her determination.*) You will. (*Still he falters; she angrier.*) You shall. (*He resists; in her a first shiver of despair.*) You MUST. (*In him, first flush of contempt: in her, desperation.*) I'LL TEACH YOU. (*He is breaking her grip on him and she knows it.*) I'LL WAIT. (*He raises one hand: she cowers.*) I'LL DO ANYTHING. (*He becomes aware of his power and looks down on her: she screams out her fall into infinite despair:*) AAAUUUUGGHHHHH

(*Snap Blackout.*)

SCENE THREE

(*Edge of the Blacklands: WRAYBURN, WYE.*)

WRAYBURN: I wanted to let you know: I have sent out Shambock in command of my entire army on a mission to ravage the Marches. They are to destroy everything that breathes or grows, and look to die themselves when they have done all they can. And I am going to join them.

WYE: Wrayburn, that is not the way to stop The Upstart, it is a gesture of fatal despair for you and all who believe in you.

WRAYBURN: Yes, perhaps it is.

WYE: You will betray the hope they had in you. And the hope that Echternacht had in you.

WRAYBURN: Yes, well, perhaps we can only shoulder so much 'hope' before we decide we have to shrug it off, to be ourselves.

WYE: You just want to die in pain, surrounded by the pain of others.

WRAYBURN: I WILL ANYWAY. I AM DOING, ALREADY.

WYE: AND YOU WILL BETRAY THE HOPE THAT *I* HAD IN YOU.

WRAYBURN: (*Snorts a dismissive laugh, turns to go. Then pauses, turns back.*) That hope was yours, not mine. (*She looks deeply into WYE: a mirror-moment. Then WRAYBURN approaches and holds out the necklace.*) Here. So that you can say of me, I gave back everything I took. (*She leaves.*) (*WYE alone. She dons the necklace, and arranges it. She considers: then, in a moment of resolve, claps her hands. GIL enters.*)

GIL: Seems like a man can't even try to be a hermit in peace, these days. I thought you'd seen and heard enough of me. Oh, I see: you have the necklace back, and you're trying out what you can do. 'Let's summon up Gil, take him away from whatever he's doing, bewilder him completely, then leave 'im to stew somewhere, that'll be good for a laugh'.

WYE: I just know how you love to lead a stable, settled life.

GIL: Yeah. Fat chance o' that with the amount of troops Wrayburn's mobilizing: however much I try to keep out of the run of things, no gettin' away from the rumble of their soldier games, and the feel that somethin's brewin'.

WYE: I know. I brought you here to tell you: I'm joining the battle. But not in any way that Wrayburn expects.

GIL: 'Scuse me, I thought that one of the principal attractions of bein' a witch was that you could be a survivor. Stay free of all the human compromises an' recrimination. I was even thinking of giving you a shout to ask if you accept blokes.

WYE: Witches have their own forms of compromise and recriminations, I can tell you.

GIL: So you want to settle a score with Mistral.

WYE: Not directly. If I were still a woman, I might even be dragged down into feeling sorry for her. But when it comes to pity, I'm proud to say I'm sheer witch. Something she no longer is, anymore.

GIL: Are you blaming yourself for letting The Upstart hatch?

WYE: Not entirely. But I will intervene.

GIL: I thought you looked for 'ways to abandon'. No dividin' yourself up for others. That's what I liked about you: you knew what you wanted an' you took it.

WYE: Yes. But the trick of being a really sharp witch, is to be constantly surprising as to what that might be. I do play by the rules. It's just that they're my own. And I love rewriting them. Now, for example. Care to join forces with me?

GIL: Hang on while I translate that into plain English. 'Care to be the daft prat who serves my purposes by creating a distraction, while I go and do something more important and more safe?'

WYE: (*Smiles.*) That shows some shrewd witch sense, I must admit. What I have in mind will be 'important' only if it works. 'Safe' is losing its appeal. Or rather, it's becoming another form of limitation.

GIL: Don't ask me to fight against the Marchmen. Curtis is back in their army, and he and I go back a long way. I can leave all that stuff to him now, thanks very much, but I couldn't fight alongside those attacking his folks.

WYE: I won't ask you to.

GIL: Right. Well, to tell the truth, I was discovering one major drawback in being a hermit: I become sick of my own company. When do we make our move, tomorrow?

WYE: Yes. But I also had a plan for tonight. I'm not one of those witches who can see to the very end of things. I never wanted to. I'll take the moment. And I have this gnawing shudder that suggests to me that this may be my last battle. If the Upstart commands Mistral's powers, hers are probably greater than mine. Come here, you mad actor. (*She puts his hand on her crotch.*) Weave some wild warmth up there into me.

GIL: Now *I* must admit: I'm surprised.

WYE: After tonight, I may never be able to ask. If I'm going to face Death, I want to be angry with his jealousy of what he wants me to give up: I want to be moist and glistening with life's defiance. So let's pitch and stretch together to find out some new colours in ourselves.

GIL: I bet you've said that before. But if you have, it doesn't matter.

(*Lights fade.*)

SCENE FOUR

(*The tower. MISTRAL is sprawled face downwards on the floor, naked. THE UPSTART stands to one side, dressing himself. The sex has been bad for both of them. He picks up her eye patch and tosses it in her direction.*)

UPSTART: Cover yourself up. (*MISTRAL, abject, feels for the patch and clamps it tremblingly into place.*) I'm glad you gave me back my sadness. It's what belongs to me. I was a fool to try and shed it. Perhaps being human involves recognizing that some things should never be realized. The prospect of them, is what inspires. But it's a mirage. I think we have been mistaken.

MISTRAL: Yes.

UPSTART: I think what they call 'satisfaction' is like a recovery. Things never come back quite the same as they were before.

MISTRAL: No.

UPSTART: We are one hope lighter. This invites us to refocus our minds, on how we should proceed.

MISTRAL: Yes.

UPSTART: This can bring our aim closer to the targets that are - right for us. (*MISTRAL weeps.*) Don't do that. I mean, it doesn't help, does it? Either of us.

MISTRAL: No.

UPSTART: I told you, I'm sad as well. But I'm trying to find what to do with the sadness. Invest it in something that isn't impossible. I think that's the best we can hope for.

MISTRAL: Perhaps.

UPSTART: I'm sorry. But I think that to try this again would involve both of us in - a loss of dignity. I don't want to inflict that on you.

MISTRAL: Thank you.

UPSTART: I'm sure we can find other ways to - help each other. That we'll both find easier. I'm very grateful to you. Don't forget that. Everything happens, in order to tell us something. About ourselves. And others.

(*MISTRAL sobs quietly as he leaves her. Blackout.*)

SCENE FIVE

(*Shrill, harrowing music. A mime by SHAMBOCK, suggesting broach, rampage and slaughter. Then CURTIS enters. He holds an object. He clutches for words.*)

CURTIS: I'm holding my child's head. I found it in the room next to his body. At first, I thought it was part of a broken doll. And I was right. That's all he is now. All he can be. Even if you stuck him back together, he'd stay a dead doll. Why did you turn him into a doll? He was more than that. There are dolls out there, who can be dolls. Children can do other things. But now he can't, and never will. Because of you.

SHAMBOCK: He got in the way.

CURTIS: Liar. You don't pull a head off accidentally. Was it your idea, or did someone tell you to do it? I'll bring his body in, and YOU can try sticking it back on. It doesn't even fit anymore, there are bits - (*His words shrivel up.*) And my wife. Half of her is still hanging from our tree, and the rest of her is - splayed out. On the kitchen table. I haven't found my daughter yet: I'm afraid to. You've made me afraid of ever seeing my daughter again. I should look in one of the other houses you've ransacked, but I don't know where to start. All the houses in the town have been ravaged by you and your kind.

SHAMBOCK: You're a soldier yourself?

CURTIS: Yes.

SHAMBOCK: Like as not, someone's said the same to you after some pillage. Or will do.

CURTIS: Do you have any family left alive?

SHAMBOCK: No. (*Pause.*) A mother. Never knew my dad. Might be you, for all I know.

CURTIS: Is that why you've done this to me?

SHAMBOCK: No. I fought 'cos I had to.

CURTIS: Liar. What I do to you, will be because I have to. But let's suppose: I fucked your mother. I'm your dad. Now say hello to your baby brother. (*He throws the head, which SHAMBOCK catches.*) Look in his eyes and explain it all to him. (*SHAMBOCK is transfixed; CURTIS ploughs into him. They fight, but SHAMBOCK escapes.*) Come back, son. You've a madman dad now, who's livin' only for the chance to beat out your eyes, gouge your whole face into one huge screaming mouth. Come here, till I pull you apart, to make you unborn.

SCENE SIX

(*MISTRAL lies face down on the floor, naked but for her eye patch. She rises, and kneels.*)

MISTRAL: I was almost happy then. I didn't feel like me. It was as if time could make things flourish, not wither. And I had the gall - no, the WILFUL MYOPIA - to think he might have seen beauty in me, in my body and my ways and my wanting him. Perhaps I wanted him too fiercely? Anyway, I should have known. I'm here as ever, back in this SELF I

126

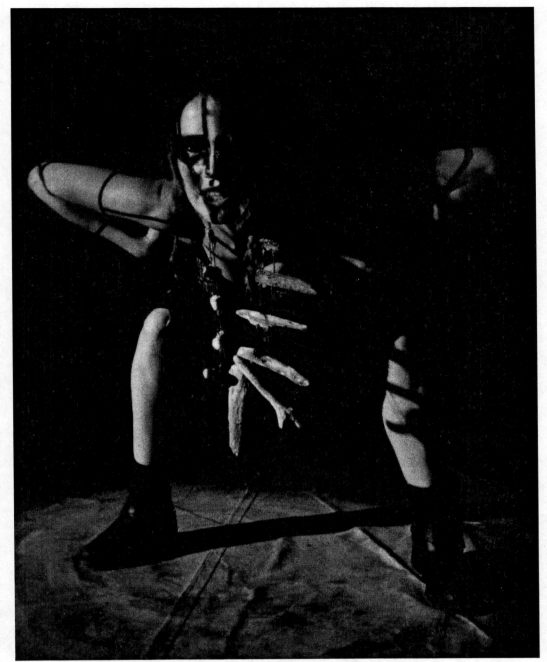

Danielle Taylor (Wye): Her incantation and dance in The Battle of the Crows.
Photo: Andy Freeman.

CAN'T GIVE AWAY, no matter how I try. Even as I reach out, (*She stands.*) I'm pulled back into this HABIT of a body, this routine of a life. Skewered with these bones, clammed up with this flesh, snapped shut with this cunt, cleft into with this mouth and peeled open with an eye that yelps its hopes so plaintively it only deserves CONTEMPT, and then this RAW PIT IN MY HEAD, unblinking idiotic open gob in my face which yawns all words to death with its implacable, unarguable, gaping DUMB KNOWLEDGE. At least it knows more than the panting, grinning foolheart that thought he could bear to look at it. I'll keep it covered forever now, in right modesty and forebearance, but I'll leave off my other garments, so they can LOOK AT THE OLD FOOL and the clothes she couldn't shed. 'Not so old, not a hag yet', the hags will jeer. But old enough and hag enough to close me off from him. So let the RAIN AND WIND PELT ME HAGGARD till the skin sags off me in flaps which pull me at last down into the ground, it might as well start now. (*She sinks to her knees.*) And let's have some brave knight to scrape out my other eye, so it won't have jump to dance across his face ever again; I'd thank him for that true man's service, best any could do now. Oh, the unpardonable SEVERANCE of this stupid, disfigured woman's body, you're the cross I'm nailed to till my tardy heart shuts up like everything else. Yes. I'll wander like this until the weathers tear me open, and find me the time to stop.

(*From up back (in unshared reality) WYE approaches, witch-blackened-vengeful.*)

WYE: Men believe that they become real by choosing death. Women paint the faces of their choices differently. Now listen to me, Upstart: you and Belia have misguided yourselves and those who would call themselves your own, levelling their souls to blackwinged tatters that feed on dead bodies and neglected seeds, and preen in stupidly elaborate show and mimicry. But now I'm rising up at you in a different black which shows a face of my own choosing and design.

(*Music. She begins an incantation. Sand spills from her fists to draw a circle on the floor. Inside the circle, she performs a strange dance.*)

I blaze and hurl out through the swirl of red caves
I'm your aisling scorpion
Come here unbidden
To show your life's more consequences than you'd WISH
I'll freeze the killers crazed to spill on both sides
And all those raising blades
Begin to turn now
Into the fury of my questioning answer

Shrink/and twist/and knot/and hunch/into/the bead/y birds/who
will/not stop/but rip/the eyes/out of/the sheep/upturned/made-
fatuous-by-their-helplessness

The crows'll plunge a ragged lunge through the clouds
Skydive a dance of sad confounded duty
The stupor-clutching drive of self-reducing men
So stir the tongue that's now unstrung in your head
Deliver twisted down
To futile screeching
And addled howling over homes denied you

Go/and whirl/around/and peck/yourselves/each oth/er in/to
death/in rage/at strand/ed selves/and bleed/your rage/to caw/and
laugh-in-madness-as-you-watch-it

And so I say so you will know from now on
That when you fly you will
Be called 'a murder'
A name to fit the blame that prompted your last shape
And in the rack and shuffle back of your brain
You'll know that I'm the one
Unstitched the statues
And crowned herself the queen of what's inside you

Of ev'/'ry man/who tries/to foul/my path/in vain/to clasp/his
fists/made feath/ers round/the name/that op/ens up/itself/into/the
breath-of-question-without-answer:

WYE! (*Sound and visual effect of appalled scattering birds.*) I'm here,
Upstart. You shan't escape me. And one of us ends here, tonight.

SCENE SEVEN

(*Music over mimes by CURTIS & SHAMBOCK, which suggest their separate subordination
and threatening; then silence, and the mimes suggest the sudden disappearance of their
adversaries. They register the silence, then speak separately to their common experience.*)

CURTIS: He - this visored machine of a man - was about to -

SHAMBOCK: Stood astride me where I sprawled, raised his axe to strike, and -

CURTIS: Screeched as his whole frame robbled down into a clot of black twitching muscle and feather -

SHAMBOCK: Shot out a caw of lost horror, winged around trying to recoil from itself -

CURTIS: Spiralled out and away, plucking and shriking at its own wizened bones -

SHAMBOCK: Loomed off, as if to split the sky -

CURTIS: But couldn't even split itself against the sky -

SHAMBOCK: Nor smear away its wings -

CURTIS: Or its skinned eyes -

SHAMBOCK: Or whatever had fisted itself up inside its guts and temples -

CURTIS: As if lost forever to itself. (*Pause.*) As are we who were left to watch it. And to go inside ourselves, to ourselves, like they have.

SHAMBOCK: (*Registering for the first time CURTIS's separateness.*) We met earlier. We were bent on deaths: others' and our own. But nearly all the troops have (*Pause.*) flown. We are two of the few who remain. Something must have saved us both.

CURTIS: Saved me for a reeling man's mind, spinning to lash me till I break. It's given me the slower poison. I'd have sooner snapped into a crow with the rest. They dimly know what they've turned into. I'm left to rake over the shards of my family, home and land, and guess what doing so will make me become. (*Enter GIL.*) You long leery stick of bad luck. Come to mouth banalities, or gloat?

GIL: No. Curtis, I'm sorry about your family.

CURTIS: Why would you be? You told me how you found it leeching repetition. You should be congratulating me instead if you were true to yourself, by the way I intend to KILL ALL CROWS, d'you see?

SHAMBOCK: Why bother?

CURTIS: Why not? Then I can REPAINT THE LANDSCAPE AND MYSELF with their innards. I find that we require - new decoration. I will do

130

what I must. (*He exits.*)

SHAMBOCK: Somewhere in the Upstart's tower, my snarlingcrazy mam's chained up. Help me find her: please.

GIL: Yes. I will. Let's go. (*They do.*)

ACT FIVE, SCENE ONE

(*The tower. VIXEN caged. Enter LONGWORTH.*)

LONGWORTH: Hello, Vixen. I came to tell you: it surprised me when Mistral changed her mind from rescuing and freeing you. That was why we originally came here, after all. But I think she's been right to keep you caged up, because it is actually for everyone's good including your own. Because everything you do just gets you and us into TROUBLE. This arrangement makes things simpler for us all. I think you ought to know that, and actually be QUITE GRATEFUL to Mistral, after all.

VIXEN: TRIPE! 'Cos I won't flounce around wittering about what's best for ev'rybody like you, 'cos I hang on to some of me old wild ways and sprack in words you've never travelled far enough to understand, you ALL THINK I'M SAFT. You're just shy of the taste of blood an' wouldn't know a cunning linguist if 'e licked yer.

LONGWORTH: But there's no need for you to do all that anymore.

VIXEN: You talkin' at me makes me want to bash my brains out right on these bars.

LONGWORTH: Actually, I do know that feeling. See! I have feelings too, which you would not credit me with, just because I don't MAKE A THING OF THEM all the time.

VIXEN: I like ter make things of 'em. Know then I've done somethin' with the day.

LONGWORTH: The question is, what can the day do with you, what way will it find for you to serve a larger purpose.

VIXEN: My own purpose does me fine.

LONGWORTH: Now, if I might dare say so, I think that's a very immature attitude in

131

one of your years. I'm glad I've understood about these things as relatively young as I have. When I have these feelings, do I bang my head, or shout about doing so? No. I bottle them, instead, with Mistral's guidance, rendering them portable (*Produces a bottle.*), convenient and quick to use in situations other than those in which they arose, ingredients in a larger, more considered spell.

VIXEN: But it's the times an' places they arise, that you should vent them!

LONGWORTH: Not entirely. You naturally speak as someone who never considered the prospect of one day rising to the level of senior sorceress - (*A crash.*) - what's that?

VIXEN: I'd get yer bottles ready.

(*LONGWORTH begins a fumbling, girl guidish check of her phials. WRAYBURN creeps up behind her and slits her throat.*)

WRAYBURN: I though witches were supposed to be formidable. I've known sleeping rabbits cause more problems.

VIXEN: Silly slip of a saint-cadet. Bottles no good to you now. Never had a chance to feel the fusin' of confusion.

WRAYBURN: And it so quiet, suddenly. Dozens of men, left dazed, where there were hundreds mad for hacking. Skies above, blotched up with birds, who burst out cawing, then fall quiet at the sound they've heard themselves make, and circle silent.

VIXEN: That so? Wye's on the warpath, then. Only her could suck up the powers to do that.

WRAYBURN: I told her to stay out of this, interfering slut! Right, where's your master?

VIXEN: Ain't got one, furrowface.

WRAYBURN: You're in a cage in the Upstart's tower, aren't you? Where is he?

UPSTART: (*Disclosed.*) Here, Wrayburn. Awaiting you. I wanted us to have you to ourselves. My association with Mistral has made me much stronger, in some ways, you see. I am so full of creation. Look here, for example: someone who wants to say hello, again.

Rob Storr (The Upstart) and Charmian Savill (Vixen): The Battle of the Crows.
Photo: Andy Freeman.

(*A masked figure approaches her threateningly. She is alerted: there is something particularly disturbing about the figure.*)

WRAYBURN: I'm not a child, to be scared by a mask - (*She plucks it away: it is ECHTERNACHT, reanimated as a zombie.*) Echternacht - oh no - oh yes - (*She extends a hand to his face, tenderly: he grabs her wrist, twists it, hits her, throws her down.*)

UPSTART: It seemed fitting to revive him. He is mine, now. He'll prove it, in you.

WRAYBURN: Never! (*Desperately, as ECHTERNACHT-ZOMBIE seizes and beats her remorselessly.*) Echternacht, it's me - every inch of me has ached to see you and hold you again - how can you do this? - don't you see me anymore? Are you just a body? I LOVED YOUR BODY! I STILL DO! You are hurting me where I SCREAM FOR YOU IN THE NIGHT! But I could love that pain. That was pangs of death and grim certainty. This is making you - and my body - so OBSCENELY ALIVE again, stop, I beg you. This is such APPALLING, WRETCHED SPITE, breaking me open in my old broken places, FOR ONCE, PLEASE, SOMEBODY HELP ME!

UPSTART: You make me wonder, Wrayburn. Is love a gratitude for the knowledge of the power you have over someone? Or a yearning to have that power?

WRAYBURN: I WANTED US TO BE MADE AND LEFT ALIVE! THAT'S THE ONE THING I REALLY WANTED!

UPSTART: But, you see, no one ever is. Echternacht taught me that. And now, I'm having him teach you. How truth kills you.

WRAYBURN: AAWWHH, KILL ME NOW. I CAN'T BEAR THIS.

UPSTART: You have wanted to die, and have others die for you. I think death always responds to such a summons, but often in a way that calls the summoners's sense into question. Do you know what is firing this pummelling of your bones and flesh and hope? It is the senselessness of this world. And now I am the King of it all.

WRAYBURN: JUST MAKE IT STOP.

UPSTART: I can't. I won't.

SCENE TWO

(*CURTIS & GIL, apart.*)

CURTIS: (*Reading a letter.*) 'Dear Curtis,
I left this with you because I didn't want to wake you today. I think
sleep is a good idea, but not at the foot of the Upstart's tower. You look
like a sentry, and might spark the siege which some survivors are
muttering about. I've met some people I have to try to help. It may be
my last chance to make myself into something that does not eventually
disgust me. You may well be angered by the company I keep, but I can
assure you that we regret what has happened to us all. Sometime
during the next twenty-four hours, if you are in our way, we must ask
you to stand aside. If you do not, you'll find out how determined we
are. You can reply by dropping a note in the dead tree trunk on the
edge of the copse opposite. We will only collect it when we've taken
every precaution to ensure you're not watching. I want to give you this
chance. Listen out. Yours, Gil.'

GIL: 'Gil,
Reluctantly, I write this reply. I no longer care if you are alive or dead.
Take every precaution you wish, but I will not be watching the tree. In
the sky or on the soil, we are all carrion now. Don't pretend you can be
anything else, whoever you're with. Stay away, leave me alone and let
me get on.
Curtis.
P.S.: I always listen. Unlike you.'

(*CURTIS tears up his letter as GIL scrunches up his.*)

             So here we are. A place to stand: must also be a place to fall.

(*WYE appears to put her hand on his head or shoulder. GIL shrugs it away and leaves her
alone.*)

SCENE THREE

(*The Upstart's Tower: VIXEN caged. The UPSTART watches, as ECHTERNACHT-ZOMBIE
holds up WRAYBURN, now resembling a limp broken rag.*)

UPSTART: Are you sorry for your life yet, Wrayburn?

135

WRAYBURN: I could be. But I've decided that even if Echternacht's fist does scuff away the last of my face, there was a time when he caressed and kissed it. And then, he was doing what he wanted to. You can make him strike, and make me wince. But you don't know what it is to give, or to accept.

UPSTART: Mistral and I have - exchanged. I found it an attempt to mask and evade the sadness which is ultimately the only thing we have, to use.

WRAYBURN: By seeking to brand it on others.

UPSTART: Don't we all? Is that not what humans do?

WRAYBURN: (*Wearied by pain.*) Yes.

VIXEN: Sights like this, as make me glad I'm not.

UPSTART: Curtis: Come up to us!

WRAYBURN: What's this, someone to wank over me while I take the next bashing? If you're planning a gang-rape, it won't be the first I've had.

UPSTART: Don't be disgusting. Curtis: I wanted to show you this. Our arch-enemy is in my power. I can't give you back your family, but this might, in part, redeem their suffering, and yours. This is what it was all for.

CURTIS: This? (*Pause.*) Have you looked outside of here? There's almost nothing left.

UPSTART: But, Curtis, this is why that had to be. Look at her, helpless. This is our victory.

CURTIS: Right. (*An effort.*) Good. (*An explosive crash as a flank of the tower is broached.*)

UPSTART: The last gasps of scattered resistance. Let them come.

WYE: (*Emerging from a billow of smoke with SHAMBOCK & GIL.*) Hello, Upstart. I'm here to be the last terrible question of your life. You're about to discover WHY you should never cross a witch.

UPSTART: Just because you give something, you feel you have the right to take it away? Do you know Mistral's transferred her powers to me? (*With a gesture, he paralyzes WYE: she gasps.*) Now let me hunt around here for the cracks in your armour. That's interesting: I can divine something in you that you're not aware of yourself. It seems that the sharpening needs of your recklessness have brought you to the point of conceiving a child inside you.

WYE: WHAT?

UPSTART: I'm not surprised you don't believe me. But it's relatively easy for my new powers to prove it to you by turning your little grub antagonistic to its host and making it start to consume you from within. (*He conducts with a gesture: WYE is promptly debilitated by a grinding, gnawing sensation in her stomach, and cries out. UPSTART approaches her in her helplessness.*) Sorry, my Black Fairy. You've let enough life slip in for now. *I'M* going to be the real live boy!

VIXEN: SSSHAMBOCK!! Burst me out, my bastard!

SHAMBOCK: Vicious freedom's comin', Mam, to hag you out.

CURTIS: (*Bars his way with a blade.*) No families any more. They're gone, like mine. We're to be broken down level now. I'll show you how it is.

GIL: Curtis, let him pass.

CURTIS: No. If you stop the Upstart, I lose the last scrap of sense inside my loss. I'm making a stand for OUR HOME, damn it! Can't you see that, you traitor?

GIL: Curtis!

CURTIS: Gil.

GIL: Curtis. (*GIL shoots CURTIS.*) Blazing hell. I've killed him. I loved that man, and his wife, and his kids. And I've just killed the last one left.

UPSTART: You wretch. You want to wreck everything, just like Echternacht.

WYE: GIL, I'M FIGHTING IT DOWN, BUT HURRY, IT'S TEARING AT ME AND ITSELF...

WRAYBURN: This isn't Echternacht. THIS ISN'T ECHTERNACHT, IT'S JUST HIS UNDEAD BODY. STOP IT, QUICKLY. (*ECHTERNACHT-ZOMBIE attacks GIL, striking him down.*)

137

UPSTART: You can't! My soldier-doll here is a monstrosity of strength no man can match.

SHAMBOCK: 'S that so? Now I know why I ain't a man. Fox inside me, too. So this a hollow puppet o' warped will, insultin' its own shape? Time to put all myself inside me, now. Death's death, whatever you make it look like: I ain't scared o' this thing, 'cos it can't want to be free, so it don't know what it's fightin' for. I do: trap's open: I'm alive with brain an' rage together, at last: an' you're dead, so I'll go through you ter let myself FREE!

(SHAMBOCK grapples the ECHTERNACHT-ZOMBIE and finally tears a bar from VIXEN's cage to use as a stake to impale it through the heart. Across this:)

GIL: *(Snapping back, to UPSTART.)*: FREEDOM: that's what you wanted, to be a real live boy you said, so why's it everything you're making comes out dead, could it be the family resemblance? Why do you curdle to death everything you reach to or look at, 'cos it reminds you of what you want to be but CAN'T? That's 'cos you can't quite SEE, Upstart, you can't quite TOUCH, you can force things dead or undead but you can't let 'em live or die, and that's what men and women do. You can't bring yourself that far off by yourself, can you? That empty silence that falls whenever you stop someone else gettin' in your way could never, ever be ESSENTIAL ISOLATION could it? If it is, then what do you have to win? Nothing, like that zombie fightin' to keep things down, but what are you lettin' UP, boyo, could you ever manage that? No, 'cos then you'd take a chance by passing the onus onto somethin' or someone other than yourself, an' that might CHANGE THINGS. It might CHANGE YOU, no, perish the thought, you've placed yourself above and apart from that, let's keep the dead alive an' make the living die, so you can go on proclaiming yourself king over and over again, forever amen, with people only watchin' you when you make 'em, so perish the thought you got it WRONG, perish the thought you're not a real live boy but a real dead boy, perish the thought that's all you'll ever be, perish the thought you're not tasting life but turnin' into Death Itself for all you approach and because of that for YOURSELF, perish the thought the only seeds inside you are those of death for others and yourself, perish the thought you could go on forever like this, unless you make yourself not - yourself, so LET PERISH THE BOY -

UPSTART: How dare you! If you'd known ABANDONMENT like me, you'd know what it is to have to make something out of your life -

GIL: You just make nothing out of other people's. CALL THAT A LIFE?

138

WHAT ARE YOU SCARED OF?

UPSTART: You're trying to make me think I'm wrong. ECHTERNACHT WAS WRONG, HE DISMISSED ME -

GIL: NO, I'd say he just demonstrated a properly impossible faith that you'd be more than what you experienced. That's life! Instead, you force limits on lives. That's death! So die, or do you lack the sense even to do that?

UPSTART: Stupid wretch, trying to hoodwink me into making weakness a virtue, NO, unlike you I have no doubts we're WINNING if you could just see it as I do -

GIL: Who's the WE? You won't bring yourself to see it like anyone else, because you CAN'T. So you'll break everything you can't own -

UPSTART: (*Grabbing his throat, hissing.*) All right. But don't try to tell me that isn't human, too. That want. That need to take. I learnt it from your sort, after all.

GIL: So go on, take my neck. Then you can make me strut about as a zombie. But you can't give it back. You can't give anything. To anybody. Except, perhaps, freedom from yourself.

(*THE UPSTART's distraction has let slip his spell on WYE, who, though weakened, can move.*)

WYE: Wrayburn! Here's something you took from yourself - (*Produces clawed Gauntlet.*) - and made others wear for you - now's the time for you to TAKE IT BACK -

(*WYE throws gauntlet across floor to WRAYBURN, who dons it. The gauntlet seems to pull her into standing.*)

WRAYBURN: Yes - it is - and this isn't for my plaguerat father - or the blundering ox of a husband he shackled me to - or the country of victims I tried to yoke - this is for me, and for Echternacht, and for the reason he would give: 'BECAUSE IT WILL BE GOOD AND THOSE WHO ARE ALIVE WILL APPRECIATE IT' - (*With an immense effort, she drags herself over to the UPSTART, skewers and unseams him with the claws.*)

UPSTART: You - idiot - you were - so like me - that's why - I knew - you were - my enemy -

WRAYBURN: Not like you anymore - I'm proving something else is real - and making sure you're not. But now you're dying! So, welcome to life, Upstart - it's everything you lose - and what you give away - (*They both sink into death. SHAMBOCK checks the bodies. GIL goes to WYE.*)

GIL: Was he right, about inside you?

WYE: There's something there, for him to have kindled into viciousness. The night before the battle, I felt this wonderful, terrible abandon, because I had a premonition that we would not come through this together - so I let slip my closest control - (*Bursts into laughter.*) not the last time it'll want to kill its mum! I could magic it away, Gil, but I don't want to! Something, someone must come out of all this.

GIL: Yes - Curtis's children lost their chance -

WYE: Let's not lose ours - (*Enter MISTRAL, her naked body Babylonishly daubed, hopelessly insane.*)

MISTRAL: I am the Queen of Loss, you see. I must present myself when I am called. And when I'm not! You've took away my wounding boy, and so my dimmest desperate hope that one day I might have made him change, come back to me and learn to love. Not impossible till now! And now the possibility curled up in Wye's fleshfolds is a cuckoo, tipped out eggs go smash and leave the yawning scream of impossibility here in mine. And that is all I have, to curl myself around.

WYE: Mistral, not even you, with all your - powers, could have changed him.

MISTRAL: I agree. But still I could have spent my life trying! How can I ever find such absorbing, blinding purpose again?

WYE: You're better free of him.

MISTRAL: Better than who? Not you, LOVED, BEAUTIFUL, WILD AND PREGNANT. Free for what? TO BE OTHER THAN YOU. Now I have my magic back, and I will have to do something because you make me find you - UNBEARABLE...

(*MISTRAL casts a spell: an effect of sound and light. GIL disappears.*)

WYE: GIL? WHERE'S HE GONE? WHAT HAVE YOU DONE WITH HIM?

MISTRAL: Pitched him far away from you, further than you'll ever find him.

Something worse than his death for you to hold onto at night: knowing that he's out there, somewhere in the world, alive, for you never to find, to have him forget and forsake you and take to others as the years pass, and for him to die without seeing you and his child again, and for you to live knowing that. At least I know where my boy is. (*She goes to UPSTART's corpse and cradles it in her arms.*) And he won't be going anywhere without me!

WYE: Oh - you - vile spit of madness! It won't give either of you life, to drive me mad with grief as well! HOW COULD YOU DO THAT TO ME?

MISTRAL: Dashed happiness is an unforgettable experience, Wye. I wanted to share some of it with you.

WYE: I DESPISE YOU TO DEATH.

MISTRAL: Good. I think I will die now with a sort of satisfaction.

SHAMBOCK: No; yer won't. (*He breaks open cage.*) C'mon out, Mam.

VIXEN: (*Prowling, murderous, free.*) Aaaahhhh! I'd scream now, Mistral, while you can. You see, I'm 'drastic actions and unpalatable extremity'. I listened to yer labellin' me out. I'm 'The Embarrassment'. I'm the 'rogue unrepresentative creature' that no one in their right mind like you fr'instance could bring themselves to be associated with. Well, now me lad's sprung me free, I'll bring myself to associate with you, my little metallic truffle, and I'll show you that however elegantly you'd like to chuck your dry life o' spite, there's a way I can find to slickersnap you open into panting panic for bits of it back.

MISTRAL: Do your worst, you batty mongrel. I'm beyond this body now. I've filled my head up with my dead boy, to suck him like a stone, till my mind wears away. No pain can prise me from that. I'll never say another word from this. (*Clamps her mouth, hums, fixes her mad eyes ahead. SHAMBOCK discretely comforts the weeping WYE.*)

VIXEN: Solemn simpletons think hearts can only break once. But I'll release you from relief, Mistral, gnaw you into knowledge, find out there inside you what you could not imagine. (*She begins biting into MISTRAL, who cannot keep from issuing a cry of pain and horror, and tries to roll, crawl, scramble away; VIXEN dogs her.*) No distance from flesh for you anymore, Mistral: now it's all you have, to be taken away. (*Action unseen: feral music peaks on the sound of MISTRAL's screaming, VIXEN's unearthly howl of triumph. Lights fade on SHAMBOCK & WYE.*)

141

SCENE FOUR

(*The same. Dawn breaking through ruins.*)

WYE: One day can hold so much. And the sun still rises!

SHAMBOCK: The crows are still circling, bewildered.

WYE: As above, so below. We're all black tatters now.

SHAMBOCK: Sounds like she's finally finished. (*Enter VIXEN, blood-besmeared from jaw outwards. She carries a heart, which she flings dripping before WYE.*)

VIXEN: I broke her words. She saw this for a moment, when I'd dug in and pulled it out in my teeth. She screamed and cried for it back. I let 'er bleed away. Then brought this, for you.

WYE: It's no use to me, or anyone, now.

VIXEN: I ain't gonna eat it. Might poison meself wi' bile.

SHAMBOCK: Will you look for Gil?

WYE: I suppose so.

SHAMBOCK: You should. Kid'll want to know, who it's father was. Believe me.

WYE: Yes, I'll look. But I won't spend my life looking. There'll be other things to do. I've been thinking about them. And telling myself that though I'll miss Gil, he could be a real PRAT sometimes. (*Manages a laugh at him and herself.*) Like the rest of us. Still a bit of a boy, for facing fatherhood.

VIXEN: They always are. That's wenchwit.

WYE: My wit ran out. Still: your boy's a sharp one. You should be pleased.

SHAMBOCK: Few people an' no government now, on either side. Wonder if people will clear their own ways, now?

WYE: They didn't last time. With King Cundah dead, the Upstart stepped into the breach, and Belia squared off against him. That's what drove Echternacht into the wilderness again. Things it's hard to be reminded of.

142

SHAMBOCK: We can do what we can, with what's left. You away, Mam?

VIXEN: Yes. But I'm always out there, on the other side of the fire. (*She is gone.*)

SHAMBOCK: Right, I'm off too. No more soldierin' for me. No more soldiers! That's a start. I'll go and lend a hand. I had a good look into the Upstart, and his zombie: I know what to avoid. And I know some of what I can do, if I have to.

WYE: Good luck.

SHAMBOCK: Give us a call if you need anything - later. Take care. (*A brief touch, and he is also gone. WYE alone.*)

WYE: (*Looks up.*) Yes, you swoop and swirl. I'll tell you what you're going to feed on, if you're quick. But this ground's thick with stories, swallows 'em whole and only quakes open to break silence and memory. Here lies a man scared of his family's life running beyond him. When they died, he lost sight of himself. Here lies a woman scared of herself, marked out her life in bottles of denial, and died for promises. Here lies a man who tried to be, but failed at creation. Here lies a woman who loved him anyway, but they couldn't rescue each other from their selves, it was too late. Here lies a man who came here a foreigner in search of fortune, but chose integrity instead. And that outlasts what others try to do with his corpse. Here lies a woman who swam pain, till she found the cleanest cruelty in love. And somewhere, but not for you, there's a man who quickens to glimpse others' insides and futures, but couldn't see into his own or mine. Perhaps you'll lead me to him! And here lies someone else (*Touching her stomach.*). Witchkid-warlock on its way to bite the world, and be bitten. I'm not breaking my necklace, nor drowning my spells, I'm going to need every one of them for both of us. So you can get used to the taste of coal, kid. I've some good stories, which you can learn to tell. And then I'll let you make your own mistakes alone, like me. So come on, you black rags, with all your wary circling and swooping theft. If you won't lead, follow me if you dare, but I'm changing the rules from now on. All those who come with me will need the courage to find new freedom, and do something with it. (*Birds answer, then the music. Houselights up as she strides off out through the audience's exit door, leaving the dead behind her.*)

Afterword: Grace and Havoc: Shape-Shifting and the Imaginative Landscape of *The Wye Plays*

Mick Mangan

Metamorphoses

Long after Ovid's tales of the transformations of gods and mortals, and closer to home, emerged the traditional English ballad of 'The Two Magicians' (Child #44). In this, a young woman, courted by a blacksmith, changes herself into a bird, a hare, a mare, a fly, a sheep, a cloud, a tree - and finally into a bed - in order to escape a pursuit which might be love or might be rape. He, no less resourceful and no less magical, becomes a bird, a hound, a saddle, a spider, a ram, a lightning bolt, the morning dew, and eventually a coverlet - and in the end he has his will. Twisting and turning through shifting shapes, the two lovers (if that is what they are) enact a ritual of chasing and fighting, of capture and escape, through landscapes in which desire remains the constant force. This erotic battle of magical transformations lies somewhere in the imaginative hinterland of *The Back of Beyond* and *The Battle of the Crows*, where shape-changing is one of the 'givens' of the narrative. And at the centre of the action is Wye, the witch, whose magic is essentially a channelling of that fluidity of forms which already exists throughout this world.

In these plays the changing of shapes is not a singular gift or affliction, as it is for Caryl Churchill's Skriker, but a very condition of being. Sometimes the changes take place in characters' surreal rememberings or fabulations, sometimes they happen before our eyes. Sometimes the shape-changing has its magical or miraculous dimension, as the boundaries of life and death, of the animate and the inanimate, of the human and the not-human, are violated: thus corpses return, zombie-like, to the world of the living, scarecrows talk, children are fathered by a cinder, and squires turn into cats. Sometimes it is the projected metamorphosis of dream or of nightmare, as when Edgar meets the Tom-self he thought he had left behind in the middle acts of *King Lear*. Sometimes metamorphosis is more humanly bloody: bodies are hacked and twisted into new shapes through the brutality of others or - as with Wrayburn - by a self-mutilation which is itself a kind of power. And sometimes it takes the form of that social metamorphosis of character which is the trademark of Shakespeare's five-act history plays (including *King Lear*), where characters metamorphose from one name

145

and identity to another, inheriting titles and roles which remain constant while their bearers change repeatedly. But these changes can be more violent, more random, than those of the history plays. They do not follow the logic of heredity and primogeniture: they have a logic of their own, in which, for example, the crippled, mutilated Wrayburn remakes herself, and reappears, transformed, as the bloody warrior-queen Belia of *Battle of the Crows*, in order to avenge (according to one account at least) 'her life and all such women's'.

Heroes

In this world of changes we are accustomed to look for heroes, to identify the still point from which we can see and make sense of the chaos of shape-shifting. In the early stages of *The Back of Beyond* some possibilities appear to remain left over from *King Lear*: but Edgar, Kent and Cordella stumble, lost, through the mythical landscape which they themselves have helped to create. Eventually, Echternacht, the mercenary turned avenger, seems to emerge as such a reference point through the very fact that he embraces change, asserting 'I split my very core with change, become the change and not the core'. He appears (replacing Edgar) as a chivalric champion at the sound of the third trumpet, and acts as guide to the escaping Wye, Gil and Curtis. But for Echternacht, as for Shakespeare's tragic heroes, to embrace the change is to risk the destruction which it brings. His final change is into a grotesque parody of his former self, the soldier-doll fighting for another man's cause.

Language

Such stories of metamorphosis demand a fluidity of language. In these plays the characters speak a range of idiolects, from the darkly comic dialect of Vixen, who will 'slink in the dark, pop up as Newblack Snoutyman, come ter sing an' nibble you awake, 'fore I snap off your head', to the serious intensity of Echternacht, or the staccato rhythms of the Upstart, or Wye's dry ironies. But across the individual voices of the characters there plays a shared sense that all these characters are speaking at the very edge of meaning. Syntax and lexis repeatedly strain against the strangeness of the world they attempt to articulate or to encompass, as the speakers struggle with the words that they know in order to try to probe a reality which they do not fully understand. Which may not be such a bad definition of poetry.

It is tempting to describe such language as 'ambiguous', and perhaps there is no better word. But if this is ambiguity then it is of a type which Empson never categorized, an ambiguity which lies at the far end of the spectrum and which ends by turning in upon itself. Strategies are attempted and repeatedly fail. Poised wit not enough: Wye finds that out. Nor is that kind of equivocation which wears the cloak of wisdom. Sheltering in a peasant's cottage, Echternacht discovers his hosts dead. It is a central scene in the narrative of the two plays. As he tries to explain their deaths to their surviving son, to help the child make sense of the apparent randomness of loss, Echternacht gives him two very different versions of what happened and instructs him 'Believe whichever version you find gives you the keenest resilience, courage and appetite for life' - and so sows the seeds of his own and the country's destruction. The child (spirit-child, it later turns out: another violated boundary) latches on to Echternacht's relativism and uses it to forge himself into the political leader who glories in the title of Upstart. When the two men finally confront each other it is too late for Echternacht to protest that there is one true story.

Endings

Both plays start with an ending, while *The Battle of the Crows*, as good myths should, ends with a kind of beginning: the beginning of Wye's quest to recover the lost Gil. Even here there is ambiguity and reservation. 'I'll look,' she says. 'But I won't spend my life looking. There'll be other things to do'. But the most telling ambiguity of all is in the image which precedes and forms the backdrop to Wye's final speech in *The Back of Beyond* (that speech which then becomes the starting point for the second play). '*A lighting change highlights the collision of gazes between WRAYBURN, poised to spring, and ECHTERNACHT, poised and questioning. In slow motion, they spring into each other, as to either kill or kiss or both.*' The violence and the sexuality which permeate these plays are inseparable: an aesthetics of eroticism and death which is true to the spirit of Shakespeare - and of the traditional ballad.

Mick Mangan is a dramatist and Professor of Drama at Exeter University.

About the Author

David Ian Rabey is Professor of Drama and Subject Leader of Theatre Studies at the University of Wales, Aberystwyth. He was born in the English Black Country, and lived in America and Dublin, and now lives in Machynlleth in Wales. He is a graduate of the Universities of Birmingham and California, Berkeley. Apart from *The Back of Beyond* (written 1994-5, staged 1996) and *The Battle of the Crows* (written 1996, staged 1998), he has written *Bite or Suck* (written 1996, staged 1997), a theatrical exploration of J. G. Ballard's novel *Crash* (written and staged 2001), and *Lovefuries* (*The Contracting Sea* and *The Hanging Judge*: written 2002, staged 2004). His roles as a performer include The Exaggerater in *Don't Exaggerate*, Carlos in *The Bewitched*, Perowne in *AC/DC*, Badger in *Bite or Suck,* and Isonzo in Howard Barker's English-language premiere production of *The Twelfth Battle of Isonzo*. His critical writings include *Howard Barker: Politics and Desire* (1989), *David Rudkin: Sacred Disobedience* (1997) and *English Drama Since 1940* (2003). He is also an Associate of Howard Barker's theatre company, The Wrestling School.

Further Reading

Rabey, David Ian, 'Liberations from the Literal, or Why I Write for Theatre', in *New Welsh Review* 43 (Winter, 1998-9), pp 77-81.

Rabey, David Ian, 'Staging *Crash*: The Sexualising of Language in Action', in *Studies in Theatre and Performance* 23, 1 (2003), pp. 41-54.

Savill, Charmian, 'Healthy Frictions of Past v. Future', in *New Welsh Review* 40 (Spring, 1998), pp 66-69.

Lurking Truth/Gwir sy'n Llechu Theatre Company

Artistic policy:
- To arrest, fascinate and seduce audiences beyond the current fear of art which is not defined by tourism and utilitarian community celebration (of what, for whom, at whose behest?)
- To demonstrate the self-renewing immediacy of theatrical performance in which language is a promise written in the air and physicality is the ballet of manifested courage.
- To achieve a production style that is appropriate to the uniqueness of the play rather than to the reassuring familiarities of theatrical convention.
- To show how complexity can, in theatre as in other matters, actually be more enjoyable and exciting than predictability, and how theatre can be a living triumph of the artificial, which is what human beings do best.
- To present new work written by the Artistic Director or exhilarating re-evaluations of major works by modern dramatists neglected in a climate of theatrical cowardice.

Besides the plays in this volume, Lurking Truth has staged Howard Barker's *Victory* (in 1986) and *Don't Exaggerate* and *The Castle* (1986), Peter Barnes's *The Bewitched* (1987), Heathcote Williams's *AC/DC* (1997), David Ian Rabey's *Bite or Suck* (1997) and, in a co-production with Iomha Ildanach and the Irish Touring Company, the English-language premiere of Howard Barker's *The Twelfth Battle of Isonzo* in a production directed by the dramatist (on tour in Ireland and Wales, 2001/2). A production of David Ian Rabey's *Lovefuries* (*The Contracting Sea* and *The Hanging Judge*) is scheduled for 2004. Management board: Ken Rabey (Chair), Alison Coleman, Karoline Gritzner (and, formerly, Patricia Duncker). Company Direction Nucleus: Roger Owen, David Ian Rabey (Artistic Director).